I0471314

You Can Make More Money

The More Money Book

Steve Long

Printed by CreateSpace, An Amazon.com Company

Dedication

This book is dedicated to

Everyone who wants to make

more money without taking a

second job, working regular hours, or

spending time away from home.

TABLE OF CONTENTS

Image mode, adjustments, image size, canvas size, image rotation, Undo, cut and paste, fill, stroke, transform, free transform, select, deselect, inverse, unsharp mask, layers, rasterize text, move tool, selection tools, lasso tool, crop, eye dropper, arrange , flatten image, spot healing brush, brush and pencil tools, clone stamp, eraser, blur, smudge, burn, dodge, sponge, text tool, magnifying glass, working with product pictures, isolating an image with complex background

eBay, Amazon, Etsy, Craigslist, getting indexed on search engines, keywords, competitors websites, advertising your websites, conversion rate, classified advertising, testing ad copy and website content, search engine optimization, seo software, free advertising, you are free to sell almost anything you like, website check list

keep a notebook and make a plan, poem, selling online fulltime, a word about selling and salesmanship, barter kings, listen to your advertising message, gone fishing, bon voyage

Introduction

"You Can Make More Money" describes why all of us need to make more money now and in the future. The book is especially needed today in 2013 when 68% of people report having problems making ends meet. "You Can Make More Money" outlines several ways to make more money without taking a second job or spending a lot of time away from home.

The book explains how people with very little money and a little extra time can make extra money from home. The ideas presented here can work for anyone as long as they are not in a coma, and have the desire and knowledge to make more money.

"You Can Make More Money" shows how to build multiple little businesses (also known as profit centers or income streams) that will make money for years to come. The author advocates establishing several new income streams per year as time allows, and how this is possible working at home in your spare time. You will learn how it is possible to set up small internet profit centers without dealing with inventory, or shipping and see how some types of profit centers practically run themselves.

If you have a job, this is an ideal opportunity to earn more money now because you can do this in your spare time. If you don't have a job at the moment this is OK as well because you'll have more time to spend developing profit centers and running your businesses.

And if you are unfortunate enough to lose your job, at least by following the advice in this book now, you'll have some other sources of income to fall back on and you will already know how to create other income streams.

In the old days a Colt .45 was said to be the great equalizer but today it is the internet. Despite the fact that our economy is in pretty bad shape we are extremely lucky today to have the tremendous research and marketing power of the world wide web.

It no longer matters where we live, how old we are, what we look like, how much money we have, or what level of education that we have. Now we can all do business on the internet and market our products nationwide, using full color advertising, and run 24 hours a day, 7 days a week without anyone on duty at the store. We don't have to be near the phone or keep regular hours. In some cases we don't have to stock, handle, or ship our products, as others do this for us. In other cases people sell our products for us and all we have to do is cash the check.

Besides describing many ideas for profit centers that you can use, this book also discusses business ideas, motivation, and information about working and at home and making more money without taking a second job.

This is not a get rich quick scheme and this book is not about getting rich at all. "You Can Make More Money" describes in detail how you can build several small profit centers, or income streams, which could each generate a few hundred dollars per month and how this can be done without spending a lot of time or money.

A few modest side businesses like this can make the difference between an easy time on planet Earth and constantly worrying about money problems and paying bills. Besides, there is a lot to be said about the thrill of getting money in your inbox!

Anyone with basic computer skills can learn to do this on their own and it doesn't take a lot of money to get started. A few hundred dollars will get you started and other profit centers can be added for one hundred dollars a year or less.

Even if you don't have a computer, or the money to get started, please don't shy away from these ideas. Every problem has a solution and we have some ideas that can help in the next few pages.

The purpose of this book is to show you new ways that you can make more money without getting a second job or working away from home. Learning to make money online gives you more than the thrill of being your own boss, it gives you the freedom to live where you like and work when you want. I hope you'll enjoy this book and decide to make some money online.

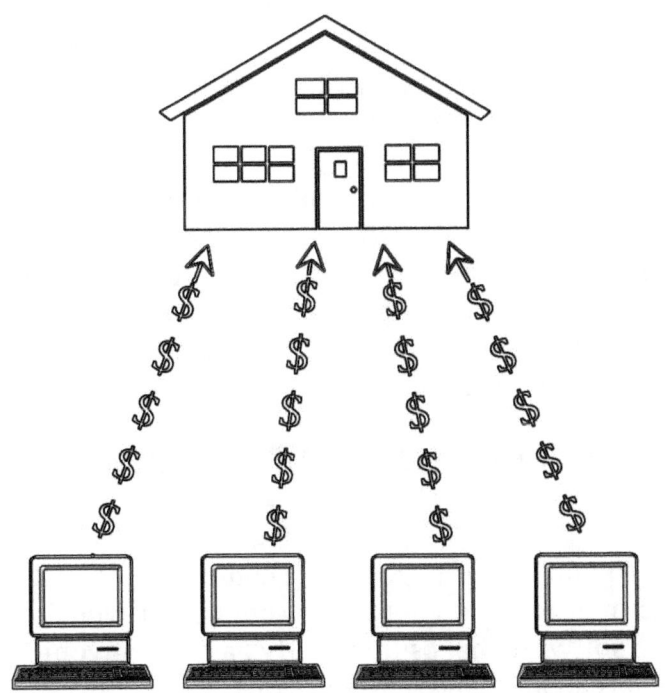

Readers are encouraged to develop
and maintain several profit center
websites, which when added together,
can produce a significant
monthly income.

Chapter 1. Q&A, The Beginning

WHAT IS AN ONLINE PROFIT CENTER?

An online profit center is a website that generates income for you. Usually this is a website that you design and operate and the site is dedicated to show and sell one or more related products. Readers are encouraged to develop and maintain several profit center websites, which when added together, can produce a significant monthly income.

WHAT EXPERIENCE IS NEEDED TO BUILD WEBSITES AND SELL ONLINE?

You no longer have to be a computer programmer to build your own profit center website. Modern software makes this pretty easy for anyone who can read and follow instructions. If you can operate a computer, send emails, surf the web, and have shopped online, then you have the basic skills to begin.

Obviously there are many things to learn but building websites is a lot easier and cheaper now than it was just a few years ago. If you are a motivated computer person you can easily learn to do this yourself and save a lot of time and money in the process.

HOW MUCH DOES IT COST?

The cost to get started is extremely low. You probably already have a place to work in your home or apartment. In addition you'll need a computer, an internet connection, and a telephone. Beyond this, it will take very little cash to start selling things online.

For about $200 you can formally organize your business as a LLC (Limited Liability Corporation), get a business bank account, a business account with PayPal, and then operate your own website (24/7) for an entire year!

Then you could add additional profit center websites as you liked for $100 per year or less. If your profit center sold drop shipped items, then the only other major cost involved in operating a web store is advertising.

WHAT IS DROP SHIPPING?

Drop shipping is when a business sells you a product at a discount and then ships it directly to the customer. The difference between the advertised price and the discount price that you pay is profit. You don't have to purchase the product before you sell it and there is no stocking or shipping when you use a drop shipper. We have listed resources to help you find millions of brand name drop shipped products to sell.

HOW MUCH TIME DOES IT TAKE?

Naturally the amount of time required to build and an operate will vary but this should give you an idea.

If you are selling drop shipped products and you have identified the products that you wish to sell then it is fair to say that a first timer could build a website over a few weeks to a month in their spare time. Once the site is up and working properly, the time required to operate it would be mostly spent forwarding customers orders to the drop shippers and following up with customers by email. This could be several hours per day if you were making lots of sales.

If you have a product like a book, DVD, or CD, you may decide to let other companies handle all the sales and the shipping so that you will not need your own website at all. But it would be a good idea to have your own site anyway for promotional purposes and then link your buyers directly to the sellers website.

In short if you can find an hour or two per day you'll be able to start and operate several profit center websites. A lot of people are pushed for time these days but most of us can find an extra hour or two per day that can be put to better use.

The average person spends this much time online and we all spend time watching more TV than we plan. Sure it takes time to start a business but unlike a conventional brick and mortar store, an online store doesn't take much time to man or maintain. If you spend as little as one hour a day learning to build and operate online profit centers then I am sure that you will be happy with the results.

I AM NEW TO COMPUTERS, WILL THIS WORK FOR ME?

Anyone can learn to build web stores and sell online but if you are a total computer novice you'll have some catching up to do. If possible, I strongly suggest that you hire a student who can teach you a lot about your computer in your home. Most kids already have these basic computer skills and most students are pretty good teachers too. Because they would be teaching you at home on your computer, this is the fastest way to get up to speed.

Computer classes are OK but they do take a lot of time and these can be confusing if using different computers and operating systems. Many people are able to teach themselves basic computer skills with books and videos but this takes some time and dedication.

Once again if you need help learning to use a computer, the $10 - $15 an hour that you might pay a student to tutor you will be a bargain.

WHAT COMPUTER DO I NEED?

You will want a fairly new and modern computer system but the brand is not important. I prefer a desktop to a laptop because of the larger screen size but both will do fine as long as you have a high resolution monitor.

If you use a laptop you'll probably need to use a mouse with it because laptop finger pads give you little control when doing image editing. This may be a problem with tablets as well.

I AM NOT A SALESMAN, CAN I MAKE MONEY TOO?

Lots of people do not believe that they are salesmen and claim that they could never sell anything. But we are all salesmen, and some are better than others. We are involved in selling everyday when we have new ideas at work to share, or when we convince the family where to go for dinner or what to watch on TV.

Fortunately for people who shy away from sales, running online profit center websites involves very little direct contact with customers so this is not an issue. Once people understand sales, they realize that being a good salesman is not about being a fast talker, instead it is about being a good listener and uncovering and countering any customer objections that keep them from making the purchase.

When selling online, observation will tell you what people are buying and which sales messages that they react to. As you listen to customers and react accordingly, sales will grow. Your customer's purchases will eventually point you in the right direction.

If you are selling sunglasses and the cheaper ones out sell the more expensive pairs, then you may choose to offer a better selection of low priced shades. If the brightly colored ones sell best, this tells you something too. If several people ask about glasses with colored lens, then you'll know that there is a demand for these and you can add them on your website. Taking the time to listen to your customers, will make you more money and a better sales person.

DO I NEED ANY EXPERIENCE TO SELL ONLINE?

Being a consumer is the most important life experience that is needed to sell online. Consumers make decisions all the time about which products to buy and what prices they are willing to pay. Since we are all consumers it is easy for us to recognize some of the factors that make us decide to buy and reach for our wallets.

If you have ever purchased anything online this is even better because sometimes the check out process works easily and other times the online purchase process is clumsy and time consuming. Both our good and bad shopping experiences will help us build better shopping experiences for our customers and lead to higher sales.

HOW CAN I DO THIS IF I DON'T HAVE THE MONEY?

One of the most attractive aspects about beginning an online sales business is that it can be done with a minimum investment of a thousand dollars or even less if you already own a computer. . This doesn't seem like much but if you don't have the money, don't let this stop you from starting a business and enjoying the rewards that will follow.

You can get creative, swallow your pride, and make an effort to get the grubstake you need in order to get what you want. It just depends on your desire to succeed.

If you don't have the money to start your own online business then I suggest finding some temporary jobs in order to earn what you need. Just open your mind and I am sure that you can think of some creative ways to earn some extra cash. It won't be fun and it won't be easy but, the good part is, it will be temporary.

Many years ago my neighbor, Mark, wrote a cookbook and decided to self publish it himself. The local printer told him that this could cost $5000 for 1000 copies. Mark and his wife had no money for this venture so they decided to bootstrap their business by doing extra work and not starting their business by going into debt.

Three or four days a week they would both get up before sunrise so that they could cut firewood before work. They would cut about a cord of wood before breakfast and Mark would drive his truck to work loaded with the wood. During the day people would see his truck and the "for sale" sign, and most days, he found a buyer so that the wood could be delivered after work.

This made them an extra $300 - $400 a week. In addition, Mark's wife did some house cleaning jobs paying $20 an hour and in a few months they had enough money to pay for the first printing of their book. The first year Mark told me that he made more money selling his book, than the President of a well-known Ivy League University!

My point is that they were willing to do a lot of hard physical work and whatever else it took to start their business. I'm sure that if you put on your thinking cap that you can find ways to earn the money that you need to begin. In case you are having trouble getting ideas, let me suggest a few that may work for you. In order to get start up capital you could babysit, wash and wax cars, do yard work, sell some of your junk, collect and recycle aluminum cans, clean houses and garages, find a part time job, do odd jobs, or handyman services, etc.

It doesn't matter what plan you choose to bootstrap and jump start your company as long as you begin the process of generating the cash that you need to begin your own business. Remember it's only temporary, and it is a means to an end. Soon you'll own your own business and you'll be the boss.

Chapter 2. We Will ALL Need More Money

This chapter is included to explain why all of us will need more money, now and especially in the future. Feel free to skip this chapter until later if you already have a strong desire to make more money without getting a second job. I have included this chapter to illustrate that we will all need more money to maintain the living standard we enjoy today.

THE NEW NORMAL:

The new normal in America today is a case of getting less and paying more. Student loan debt is now higher than our national credit card debt and many graduates cannot find work. Some have no choice but to live with their parents. For the first time in history most Americans no longer are on course to achieve more of the American Dream than their parents. More elderly people than ever are remaining in the work force despite low paying jobs because they have no way to pay their bills.

Hope for the future is at an all time low in America today and Low Expectations are rampant with world wide economic growth expected to be only about 2% a year or so for the next 10 years!

It is no secret the world around us has changed from the world that we knew when we grew up. Until recently Americans could count on getting a good job if they had the skills and education. But this is not the case today. Our parents and grand parents could reasonably

17

expect to stay with the same employer for their entire career if they wished. But this is no longer true either. Many people used to buy a new car every 3 – 5 years but this is now a thing of the past as well for the average American.

A 2013 study by Affordability Study Interest.com concludes that the average new car now costs $30,000 with a $550 a month payment. They concluded the study and stated that the average American can no longer afford to buy a new car!

Home ownership is only a dream for many and obtaining a job that will do much more than pay the bills is a thing of the past for most.

I could go on with illustrations and statistics about how economic policies have crippled our country and how are our leaders from both parties are contributing to our destruction, but this is not my point. Most of you realize this anyway. The purpose of this Chapter is to point out that we are all in the same boat and will have to learn to live with stagnant wages, a slow economy, and rising prices and out of control taxes for a long time to come.

This does not mean that we are all doomed to live with less or that we cannot achieve our dreams. It means that we will all have to work harder, work smarter, and work longer to get what we want. For many just making ends meet is a problem now and hopefully some of these people will use this book to their advantage. And for the rest of us, we are all going to need more money to survive the NEW NORMAL economy in the near future.

Some people that are making good money (often called the rich) might think that somehow they will be able to weather the economic storm of slow growth, rising prices, and taxes and that most of the hardship will be limited to others. But nothing can be farther from the truth. All of us have suffered during the slowest and most miserable economic recovery in our nation's history.

We basically have three economic classes in America today. We have a permanent Welfare Class, a Working Class to include the working poor, and the Rich who we are taught to both scorn and admire.

The Rich either own a highly profitable business or they are large stockholders in blue chip corporations with worldwide markets. They don't get paid wages and do not pay payroll taxes and are largely unaffected by a down economy like the rest of us.

The growing Welfare Class sees no desire to work when they get so many benefits for not working. Unfortunately many are trapped in this situation and most likely will never escape the cycle of dependency and slavery that results from being paid not to work.

The rest of us are in the Working Class and we will all be hurt the most by rising prices, a weak economy, and punishing taxation. Just because we have a job today does not mean that we will have the job in the future so we cannotdepend upon this to last. Many working people today are just one or two paychecks away from bankruptcy and/or foreclosure.

The simple fact is that we will all need more money in the future, if not now. This is a good reason for us to build multiple independent income streams as quickly as possible. Price hikes and higher taxes will be coming our way from every direction and prudent people will make an effort to plan on this fact and start to prepare for the NEW NORMAL without delay.

The following are some of the many factors that will require us to make more money if we are to enjoy the same standard of living that we have in America today:

1) Rising Costs under ObamaCare
2) High Gasoline and Diesel prices
3) New and Higher Taxes
4) Slow Economic Growth
5) Even Higher Government Spending
6) High Unemployment & Disability
7) Rising Cost of Food
8) More Public Bailouts for natural disasters
9) Possible Military Conflicts
10) The Next "Crisis" requiring more new laws and additional government spending.

OBAMACARE:

Obamacare related health care cost increases are just beginning to be understood. There are 15,000 pages in this law and the IRS just released its guidelines for acceptable health care plans for the 2014 tax year. The minimum health care plan that the IRS will accept is called a Bronze Level Plan. It is expected to cost $20,000 per year for a family of 5. How many families of five have you ever known that could afford this? If a family does not buy a Bronze Level health insurance plan, the penalty in this example is $200 a month. So they would have to pay over $1600 a month in insurance premiums if they wanted health insurance or pay the $200 a month penalty (and have no insurance to show for it).

Some people are not concerned about this because they currently are covered with a health care plan through their employer but many existing plans will not qualify and the ones that do will be taxed up to 40%. If you have a private health care plan, you probably have already been notified that your premiums are going up even before the law takes full effect and future raises in premiums are sure to follow. Many employers with more than 50 employees will be forced to pay larger fines and no longer give their employees health care benefits because of the enormous cost increases. Left without company health care, employees will have to choose between hardship insurance rates or going without insurance and paying the fines that are scheduled to increase annually to punish people who refuse to comply.

The law was supposed to be designed to save us money and provide universal health care for all but it will have the opposite effect. By forcing the insurance company to write poor risk policies for people with pre-existing conditions and limiting the rates that the companies can charge, the system has no alternative but to fail. Sure the health Insurance companies will thrive in the short run but eventually they will all go bankrupt. When this happens the Government will recite the mantra that business is bad and only the Government will be able to save us by giving us all Medicare coverage and taxing us on their gift. For these reasons health care costs will be going through the roof unless Congress gets some brains and some spines to go with them.

HIGH FUEL PRICES:

Another sure sign that prices of just about everything will continue to rise is the GASOLINE PRICE that has more than doubled over the last four years. When asked about this the President joked that a new high gas mileage car would make up for the higher fuel costs but how many people now can afford a new car to save on fuel?

Obviously the price of Gasoline and Diesel influences the delivery and manufacturing costs of everything we buy. When fuel prices go up and stay up, this cost must be passed along to the consumer. Since so many people have long drives to work, this is a big weekly expense increase and consumers have no choice but to cut other spending to pay for fuel to get to work.

TAXES:

Taxes have gone up already and will be going up some more. Anyone who doubts this hasn't looked at their pay stub lately. Both political parties have refused to cut spending so higher taxes will be the rule. Higher Taxes will not be limited to the Federal Government but State and Local Governments as well. New taxes will come from every direction and higher taxes rates will be a reality for everyone.

Some people don't seem to care because about half of Americans do not pay Federal income tax. But for some reason these folks think that other people should pay more taxes even though they pay nothing. Unfortunately this group includes about half of our registered voters and they are likely to vote for higher taxes for everyone else and more government benefits for themselves.

In 1913 there were 400 pages in our nation's tax code. Today there are 73,954 pages of tax code which if placed end to end, would span 13 miles! We are taxed from so many directions that this number can't even be counted. Nobody can escape the higher taxes that will further impact everyone including those who currently skip out of paying Federal or State taxes.

Remember the lyrics to the Beatles' song "Taxman"? Notice how true these words sound today.

"Taxman"

"Let me tell you how it will be
There's one for you, nineteen for me
'Cause I'm the taxman, yeah, I'm the taxman

Should five per cent appear too small
Be thankful I don't take it all
'Cause I'm the taxman, yeah I'm the taxman

If you drive a car, I'll tax the street,
If you try to sit, I'll tax your seat.
If you get too cold I'll tax the heat,
If you take a walk, I'll tax your feet.

Don't ask me what I want it for
If you don't want to pay some more
'Cause I'm the taxman, yeah, I'm the taxman

Now my advice for those who die
Declare the pennies on your eyes
'Cause I'm the taxman, yeah, I'm the taxman
And you're working for no one but me."

by the Beatles

Here are SOME of the taxes we Americans pay each year in addition to Federal and State Income tax:

Accounts Receivable Tax, Building Permit Tax, Capital Gains Tax, CDL license Tax, Cigarette Tax, Corporate Income Tax, Court Fines (indirect taxes), Dog License

Tax, Federal Unemployment Tax (FUTA), Fishing License Tax, Food License Tax, Fuel permit tax, Gasoline Tax (42 cents per gallon), Hunting License Tax, Inheritance Tax Interest expense, Inventory tax IRS Interest Charges (tax on top of tax), IRS Penalties (tax on top of tax), Liquor Tax, Local Income Tax, Luxury Taxes, Marriage License Tax, Medical Equipment Tax, Medicare Tax, Property Tax, Rain Tax, Real Estate Tax, Septic Permit Tax, Service Charge Taxes, Social Security Tax, Road Usage Taxes paid by truckers, Sales Taxes, Recreational Vehicle Tax, Road Toll Booth Taxes, School Tax, State Income Tax State Unemployment Tax (SUTA), Telephone federal excise tax, Telephone federal universal service fee tax, Telephone federal, state and local surcharge taxes, Telephone minimum usage surcharge tax, Telephone recurring and non-recurring charges tax, Telephone state and local tax, Telephone usage charge tax, Toll Bridge Taxes, Toll Tunnel Taxes, Trailer registration tax, Utility Taxes, Vehicle License Registration Tax, Vehicle Sales Tax, Watercraft registration Tax, Well Permit Tax, and the Workers Compensation Tax.

Other new taxes that are likely to become realities are a Value Added tax, an Internet tax, and the scariest of all, the Carbon tax which is somehow supposed to keep the climate from changing. The point here isn't to get political about taxes. More taxes are being legislated all the time. They are here to stay and there is nothing that can be done to change this. Taxes, all kinds of taxes, are going up and there is nothing that we can do to change this so we must plan accordingly and either make more money or learn to live on less.

SUPER SLOW ECONOMIC GROWTH:

Slow economic growth has been forecast for the next few years. The White House projected growth rate for 2014 is only 2.4% and not likely to improve for years. Russia projects a 2.4% GDP growth rate for 2013 as well. The U.K has projected growth rates in the 2% range for the next 10 years.

Please don't let the recent high marks in the stock market fool you into believing that our economy is on the road to recovery. The Dow Jones Industrial Average is only a little higher than it was in 2009. Our Federal Reserve is buying bonds at the rate of $82 Billion a month to keep this party going and the Chairman announced that this policy will continue until the economy improves. Japan has announced it will begin doing the same thing on a massive scale.

Robust growth does not appear to be around the corner here or elsewhere in the world. Without a better GDP growth rate to bring in more revenue to the Treasury, taxes and deficits will continue rise in an attempt to feed the growing government demand for cash.

I'm sure that you have heard the saying that figures never lie but liars figure. This is certainly true for governments. The numbers get "adjusted" all the time. Americans know that we have inflation but this is not the case according to the government because food and energy price hikes do not carry much weight in their formula. The way we calculate GDP is changing so our economic recovery will look better than it is. Unemployment numbers are fudged all the time and are not even close to reality.

It would be illegal for a public company to use

the accounting practices used by our government. This is because our near $17 Trillion deficit does not include unfunded liabilities like retirement pensions and social security. How large of deficit would this be? Nobody wants to know. It is just easier to ignore it altogether.

EVEN HIGHER GOVERNMENT SPENDING TO COME:
This year in 2013 the Federal Government had record tax revenues of $2.7 Trillion but ran a deficit of over $1 Trillion. The Office of Management and Budget predicts $1 Trillion deficits for the next 10 years. This would put our National Debt on track to reach $30 Trillion in 10 years without adding the additional expected $4 Trillion in Immigration Reform Bill costs. If and when interest rates climb much of the money our country spends will be to pay interest only payments on this debt. Now interest rates are historically low but when they rise again, this will be a huge problem.

Another way to look at the National Debt is to view this as unpaid taxes with accumulating interest.

The major component of Federal Government Spending is the entitlement programs like health care, pensions, social security, welfare, food stamps and unemployment compensation. During peacetime, Defense spending is the second highest spending category followed by Interest (on the national debt) and infrastructure and services, which basically includes everything else and often referred to as discretionary spending. This includes education, fire, police, the criminal justice system, physical infrastructure, transportation, science, research, and other government expenses for payroll.

26

HIGH UNEMPLOYMENT RATES RECORD DISABILITY PAYMENTS:

Unemployment rates continue to stand in the way of any hope of recovery. So many people have dropped out of the workforce that the official jobless rate has been skewed to show only 7.6 % although the real number is much higher. The labor participation rate is the lowest since 1979 at 63.3% since so many people have stopped looking for work or retired from the workforce.

In addition 8.8 million Americans, a new record, are collecting federal disability payments. Today we find that there are 13 Americans with full time jobs for each person collecting a disability check. Since disabled people would pay little or no federal taxes this burden must be carried by fewer tax payers and continued high taxes. Anyone who works for wages can expect even higher payroll taxes to come.

THE RISING COST OF FOOD:

Food costs are going up and this is apparent to anyone who does their own grocery shopping. Sometimes the reasons for price hikes are due to droughts affecting crops like soybeans and corn. Other price increases can be blamed on increased regulations or down sized packaging.

News stories affect food prices as well. In fact the Pink Slime story destroyed an industry and raised meat prices for everyone. Hamburger that used to sell for $1.80 - $1.99 per pound now is over $3 per pound since what the press called pink slime is no longer included. With production and transportation costs going up food

27

prices will surely follow.

MORE PUBLIC BAILOUTS FOR BAD WEATHER:

More bad weather events are a certainty in the future. We all understand that sometimes it rains and sometimes the wind blows. Sometimes these storms are so wide spread with so much damage that only the Federal Government can help.

The problem is that now our Government is expected to kick in lots of cash to help with storm relief and we cannot afford to do this forever. No matter how much money is handed out by the Feds the areas are seldom rebuilt and the area is devastated for years to come. We spent over $200 Billion on Katrina and much of the coastline looks like a war zone today. Recently we spent $60 Billion on hurricane Sandy and you can expect the same result.

Obviously we will continue to have bad weather events in the future and, like pain and suffering awards, the cost to the taxpayers will continue to rise.

MILITARY CONFLICTS:

If history is any indicator, we are likely to continue to use military force throughout the world and spending money that we do not have. We have already announced that we will prevent Iran and North Korea from expanding their nuclear capabilities so war could easily be in the cards.

Even without a new war our defense spending is off the charts since anytime after WW2 and currently this is our second highest category of federal spending behind pensions, healthcare, and welfare. The high cost of high tech weapons to replace boots on the ground and our obligation under the Constitution to provide for the common defense suggests that we should expect to spend a large part of the budget on defense in the future.

ONE NEW CRISIS AFTER ANOTHER:

It seems that one new crisis after another surfaces and TV coverage captures our attention, our hearts, and purse strings. Politicians rely on this so each new crisis is an opportunity for the government to issue new regulations, spend more money, and play to the camera.

No matter what the crisis, the solution according to Congress is to throw more money at it, then declare victory, and go home for the weekend. No matter what, we are stuck with Leaders and Representatives in both parties who will continue massive amounts of government spending as long as we are dumb enough to continue to allow them to keep their jobs.

THE GOOD NEWS:

The good news is that even though millions of people are out of work, lots of people still have jobs and are spending money online. Online sales are predicted to grow by 10% a year for the next five years.

MORE GOOD NEWS:

The other good news is that today nearly everyone has access to the world wide web, the greatest money making opportunity the world has ever known. This book will show you how you build small internet profit centers or virtual storefronts that will keep making you money month after month at a very low cost.

Some products you may choose to sell require you to make shipments to customers but other businesses require very little effort once set up, other than cashing the checks.

You can set up as many profit centers as you wish and live anywhere that you can access the internet. Your age, income, education, appearance, or health does not matter to anyone online. With the information presented in this book you can make more money without getting a 2nd job or working away from home.

FOR THE SAME AMOUNT OF
MONEY THAT MOST PEOPLE
SPEND ON COFFEE EACH DAY,

YOU CAN HAVE YOUR
OWN PROFIT CENTER WEBSITE!

Chapter 3. You Can Make More Money without getting a 2nd job

At one time my Father was a high level official in the Treasury Department and he was telling me about a meeting that he attended. Someone from the academic world was commenting that people rose to a certain level of economic success in life and that generally speaking they could not rise above this to begin making more money.

When I heard this it immediately did not ring true to me. Unless someone is in a comma I thought, anyone can certainly make more money. It might not be as much as they like, doing the work that they like, at the time of their choosing but they can make more money. What was this guy talking about? It didn't make sense to me.

People can babysit, shine shoes, wash cars, walk dogs, wash windows, and the list goes on. If someone is healthy there is no reason that they can't make more money if they want to and if they are willing to work for it.

It is true that most people who have a job and a family life feel that they do not have the time or energy to make more money. If anything they feel that they need to relax, and that any time they spend doing so is well-deserved and good therapy at that. Most people with full time jobs are busy with their lives and not motivated to try to make more money. They are tired and soon realize that they must try to live as much as possible within their means.

As long as people think their checks will keep

coming, regardless of how much they make, the natural tendency is to spend a little more. We commonly buy larger and more expensive homes than we need and the same is true of cars.

This large debt practically guarantees that we will do everything possible and do our best to keep our jobs. Our jobs consume most of our time and energy. And our days off are often spent catching up on sleep or busy with projects around the house. Even if we wanted to find a better job there is little time left in the week to look for other positions and go through the application and interview process.

Once people reach a level where they can pay the bills, they often stop trying to improve their lot in life. Maybe this is what the man at the Treasury Department meeting was talking about. People weren't held back at all, they just stopped trying to make more money and did their best to enjoy their lives and families and live within their means.

In the past making more money generally meant getting a better paying job or getting a second job. Ask anyone with two jobs what this is like and they will tell you that they don't have a life. They are trading their hours for a handful of dimes and it is hard to understand how they can do this. When asked they will tell you that they have no other choice. They have bills to pay and a family to support.

But today we have many more options to make additional money than ever before. Sure we can still trade our time for wages but we only have so much time. Besides all work and no play is not the formula for a healthy or happy life.

If someone has money they can invest this in stocks, real estate, or income producing assets. But most working people do not have money so what options are available for them to make extra money without taking a second job? It is the purpose of this book to present some viable options for people to make extra money from home.

The types of businesses and marketing strategies that I present here, are not limited to people with college degrees or special skills. Age, sex, race, weight, physical condition, or appearance will not be a factor in whether you succeed or not since you won't be dealing with customers in person. You can do this work in your underwear if you like, it won't matter.

The profit center ideas presented here will not require a lot of money to initiate and you can continue operating them for years to come. When and if your profit centers stop producing you can always start another to replace it.

One of the unusual aspects about this book, is that it does not promote the idea of getting rich quickly or otherwise. Most money making books on the market today want the reader to THINK BIG and start a business or company that will someday become an family empire. However "You Can Make More Money" promotes the idea of THINKING BIGGER by THINKING SMALL. This approach advocates starting and operating several small profit centers which can make you a few hundred dollars a month each. Once one business is set up and running smoothly another different business can be started so that in a few years, you have a diverse collection of small profit centers each producing additional income for you. THINKING SMALL allows you to start these businesses with little effort, low cost, and little risk.

Creating profit centers like this can be done from

home in your spare time or eventually be expanded so these income streams replace your job entirely. These businesses can be started with very little money often with only a few hundred dollars. If you don't have any extra money to do this see the last chapter for some ideas to help get you started.

You will need a computer and an internet connection and chances are that you have this already. If you do not have a computer, you can buy a used computer system for a few hundred dollars and for a little more, even get a new one. Learning to use a computer is an investment in time. If you need some coaching, there are a lot of high school kids that are willing to help for modest wages and they make excellent tutors. The truth is that the help menus and tutorials included with modern software make it fairly easy to learn the basic features of most modern computer programs without outside instruction.

Almost all businesses require regular hours and monitoring of your store or telephone during business hours but this one does not. Your online profit centers can be selling for you 24 hours a day, seven days a week, so all you have to do is answer emails, fill the orders, and cash the check. If you like, you can have the shipping handled by someone else and it is possible to never touch the product at all.

You will learn how to find good products to sell and what types of products sell online. We will show you the best types of products to choose for long term potential sales. Also we will present ways to make your your own web site without programming experience and how you can own your own domain and have it hosted for about 50¢ a week. Imagine having your own online storefronts for only couple of dollars per month. It's amazing.

YOU CAN MAKE MORE MONEY

Regardless of the state of the economy, most people are working and spending more and more money online. The world wide web is the best opportunity right now for the average person to start their own business and make extra money today.

I will share some ideas to help you promote and advertise your products cost free and discuss some things you should know about business and taxes to help you get off to a good start.

Lots of people are making money online these days and with the help of this book there is no reason for you not to join the party. Besides, making money with your wits is fun and if you look at it this way, it won't be like work at all.

With very low cost you will be able to find some ideas for profit centers that work for you. If an idea doesn't work for you simply try another.

After awhile you can own and operate a small portfolio of online profit centers that each pay you on an ongoing basis. When added together, several small profit centers can produce a significant monthly income.

New Ideas are terrific,

But without your energy,

and your action,

the Ideas can never

make money for you!

Chapter 4. Finding Good Ideas for Your Online Profit Centers

Almost anything that you can imagine is sold online and taking the time to choose a good product or idea for your profit center is important. Obviously any item you sell should be of good quality but other considerations are:

1) The item should be easy to pack so that it can be shipped without damage.
2) It should not be too heavy so that shipping costs are low. This is especially important if you offer free shipping as an incentive to buy.
3) The item should be familiar and not need a complicated explanation about how it works
4) People must have shown in the past that they are willing to buy similar items online
5) The item must be priced competitively and still make a profit after all sales costs.
6) Ideally the product can be drop shipped from the supplier or manufacturer so that you do not have to do this yourself. Drop shipping also insures that you don't have to tie your money up in inventory and that you only buy an item after it is sold.

Some of the best products are protected by Patent or Copyright Law so that direct competition is all but eliminated.

1. BOOKS, eBOOKS, AND Dvds MAKE GREAT PRODUCTS FOR YOUR ONLINE PROFIT CENTER:

Books, DVD's, and eBooks are some of the Best Product Ideas that I can suggest for anyone.

a) These are protected by Copyright Law.
b) They can be easily shipped directly from the publisher for a low cost.
c) People are used to buying books, videos, and plans online.
d) You don't need an inventory because these can be printed and shipped as needed.
e) There is a low investment cost with on demand publishing often only a few hundred dollars so that anyone can afford to do this.
f) e Book sales generate very high royalties compared to the royalties that are generated with print book sales.
g) Books and DVDs can generate income for many years to come. Many books continue to sell for twenty years or more.

Please don't dismiss the idea of writing a book or making a video because you have no experience. This is a lot easier than you think and chances are that you have some knowledge that people want. You don't have to be a great writer to write something that sells. "How To" books are fairly good sellers and, as long as the author knows what he or she is talking about and communicates this effectively, the public will be happy. Besides nobody ever returned a book or asked for refund because they didn't like the content or writing style.

YOU CAN MAKE MORE MONEY

In terms of sales, fiction and non-fiction books seem to be about even. In order of popularity the best fiction genre is crime, followed by science fiction at 26%, literature with 24%, and romance capturing 21% of the market. Non-fiction genre sales rank as follows with history at 31%, biographies29%, spirituality 26% with the remainder split between self-help, current affairs, true crime, and other non-fiction.

People are hungry for real life How To information that you already know. Since many people do not learn well by reading, DVD instructional videos are perfect for them. With modern software these are pretty easy to put together so that they are good enough to sell.

Copies of your master DVD or eBook can be made easily and sent to customers online to avoid shipping costs and delays.

You might not think that you have anything to show or say that people would buy, but I'll bet that you are wrong. If you know how to trim rose bushes or fruit trees, there are plenty of people who don't. If you know how to fix a Volkswagen or a Lawn Mower, there are plenty of people who don't. If you know how to make a good piecrust, there are plenty people who would like to learn. Practically any how-to skill subject material can be presented in print or video and sold online.

For some reason there are lots of people who buy information just in case they will need it later.. A few years ago "Organic Gardening Magazine" offered cold frame plans for sale. About 90 people bought the plans, and in a follow up survey, the magazine found that only one person actually built the cold frame, a kid. The others paid for information that they might want later on and put it on the shelf. This is more common than you would think.

A few years ago if you wanted to write a book and get it published you would have to find a publisher willing to take a chance on you and your work. The only other alternative was to pay a publisher to print copies of your book and this was costly, often $5,000 or more for the initial printing. And then it was up to you to sell the books yourself!

But now we have a variety of on demand publishers to choose from. The cost to produce a book varies due to size, paper, number of pages, number of images, etc. but you can get a book printed using a company like this for a few hundred dollars depending on size and options.

There are several companies that do this but I have chosen to publish this book using CreateSpace.com

They make the whole process easy and have a direct relationship with Amazon.com so that your book is not delayed getting to the Amazon.com customer both in the U.S and in Europe. In addition they make it easy to convert your print book format to an eBook so that your book will be available in Kindle format.

Offering your book in Kindle format is important because customers can get your book without delay. It is also important because you will make more money if you sell your book as an eBook.

To give you an idea how significant this is I should tell you that I had a book deal with a small publisher. The book sold for $14.95 retail and my commission was $1 per copy for any books they sold at retail. However most of the books were sold at deep discount wholesale prices of about $3 each so my commission on these books was only about 30¢ per book.

YOU CAN MAKE MORE MONEY

According to the royalty calculator on the CreateSpace.com website the royalty for a 6" x 9" book with a black and white interior with 160 pages priced at $15 retail would be as follows: $6.23 if sold through Amazon, $3.23 if sold through expanded distribution, and a whopping $9.23 if sold as an eBook through their eStore. They print the book, dub the DVD, sell it for you and send you a check. This is American Capitalism and Opportunity at its best. In 2012 eBooks were 22.5% of total industry book sales nationwide and this is a trend that cannot be ignored. eBooks are a great opportunity for anyone with something to say or share.

It is hard to say how long it takes to write a book. It depends a lot on whether you know what you want to say. I think it is reasonable to say that you can write a How To type book in as little as three to six months if you write a little everyday. Thanks to the internet, research is easier than ever and the same can be said for word processing programs.

The best advice that I can give to anyone who is writing a book it to work at it a little each day and don't impose an artificial deadline on yourself. If it takes six months instead of three, then that is what it takes. The next best advice I can give about this is to give it another 30 days after you are finished to really fine tune the manuscript and make it as error free as possible.

I have never created a novel so this writing style is completely foreign to me and I would expect that this would take more time than writing about familiar subjects and experiences. The bottom line is that it takes what it takes. Whatever time it takes to create a book or eBook will probably be worth it.

In any case I cannot stress enough how books, eBooks, and DVDs are perfect product ideas for profit centers and I hope you take the time to become a published author. These items are protected by copyright and easily manufactured as needed without you having to purchase and stock inventory or engage in shipping. Products like these can be produced and shipped by others so all you have to do is promote the product and cash the checks.

2. SELLING DROP SHIPPED ITEMS ONLINE FINDING A NICHE MARKET:

Besides Books, eBooks, and DVDs you might wish to find products that you can buy wholesale and re-sell at a profit online. There are millions of brand name items that you can sell at a markup and the company will drop ship the item directly to the customer.

One place to look is Doba.com. They have 1.4 million products to choose from. The idea is that members can find products to buy at wholesale prices and resell at a markup. Then people can sell the brand name products that they like via their own web stores and online auction sites. . When a customer pays for an item, you would contact Doba.com and place an order for the item. The item would be shipped directly to the customer and you would pocket the difference between your retail price and the Doba price. (see more drop shippers that are listed in the Resource Section at the end of this book).

The advantage of doing business through a drop shipping company like this is that you don't have to buy any inventory until you make the sale and have been paid. Also they handle the shipping for you and this is a big plus since shipping takes lots of time.

A disadvantage about using a drop shipper is that you lose contact with your customer and must depend on someone else to get the order shipped promptly so that it arrives without damage.

Many people are doing well and building their business around drop ship products from companies like Doba. I am certain this is a great way to build a small profit center although it takes more daily management time to do this than writing one book or DVD and letting someone else sell it. It appears that their most successful sellers operate on a 10% - 20% profit margin. This isn't bad for something they only order after they sell it and have the money in hand!

It is important to understand that customers see through and resent over-charging on shipping. I mention this because some sellers view shipping charges as additional profit centers and customers are fed up with this practice. Because of this I suggest that you limit shipping charges to something close to your actual cost, or better yet, find a way to include this in the price if you can.

The experts advise that to succeed in this business it is important to sell what you know and then choose you niche market accordingly. Following your heart and selling what you know is especially good advice when it comes to selling online.

If you like music, then you could feature some quality products that you like, and chances are that others will like them too. Letting your interests be your guide is the best way to be sure that your online profit center store is unique so that buyers will remember you and suggest your store to others or buy again.

Also it is important to offer your customers more than just the lowest price in town. If you have ever thought about running a virtual store, take a look at Doba.com, Product Sourcing.com, and some of the other drop shippers listed at the end of this book in our Resource Directory and also on this free webdirectory at dropshipsites.com/dropship_suppliers/. You'll be amazed at the deals you find on brand name items that you can sell.

3. SELLING YOUR HANDMADE ITEMS ONLINE:

In our younger days my wife and I spent about fifteen years making and selling wooden toys. We made the toys at home and traveled to art shows and sold our toys at retail. Because we were young and had a lot of energy we were able to make this work as long as we sold the toys in person. Rising fuel prices and high motel costs made traveling to shows less and less attractive and then we quit traveling to shows altogether.

As the internet became more and more popular with shoppers we tried selling our toys online, mostly without success. We had our own website with animated demonstrations but for us, internet toy sales were a bust.

Next we stopped making our regular line of toys and made political toys instead, using computer images of modern politicians. These sold much better online than our old toy line toys and we continued making these for several years until we retired from making these as well.

From my experience most handmade items are not good items to consider for an online profit center. One reason for this is that making items by yourself is a lot of work. The idea behind the profit center is to set something up that will pay off monthly without it being a lot of work. If you are spending your time making a product then you'll have less time and energy left to sell it and selling is the key. Without sales any business enterprise will fail.

One of the problems with selling handmade items online is the lack of a standard appearance in the product due to slight differences in materials. This may require a unique photo for each and every item. Another problem is that most people who produce handmade items cannot afford to heavily discount or wholesale their work.

One more reason for not getting involved with selling handmade items online is that there is always someone somewhere who will copy your item and sell it for less. This makes it difficult to get the retail prices for your work online that you may be used to if you sell your work at shows.

One last thing to consider when selling handmade items is that you will have to do all packing, and shipping. It might not seem like much time or effort to wrap something up and take it to the Post Office or shipping center but this really takes a lot of time.

I am sure that you are familiar with the saying that there is an exception to any rule, so if you have an item that you would like to try to sell online, I absolutely encourage you to give it a shot. It won't cost much to test the market and learn if there is a demand online for your work or not.

Note that I am not suggesting that handmade items do not sell online. I am just saying that other types of items would be a better choice for most people.

I remember getting an order for about 600 of our rocking politicos. These were about 4 inches high and consisted of a stained wooden base with a curved bottom that supported a wooden political figure with a freely swinging head. When you gave it a nudge the toy would rock back and forth and the politico would swing his head side to side.

I remember this order so well because we had to rush to build 600 or so rocking politico toys in less than a week. It was hell cutting out, sanding, and staining all those rockers at once and these had to be completed and dry before the rest of the toy could be assembled, packed, and shipped. I also remember that the customer was in such a hurry that all the toys had to be shipped 2nd day air and the shipping was over $300. Sure it was over a $2000 order via the internet but because the customer was in such a rush, it took a lot of fun out of the deal and we were zombies for about a week after we shipped the order.

Later we found out the reason that the buyer was in so much of a hurry, the toys were gifts intended for every member of Congress and a few other Washington officials. The only reason that the buyer found us and we made the sale was because of the internet and our website.

4. SELLING YOUR FINE ARTWORK ONLINE:

Today there are many opportunities to sell your artwork online. Like writing, these are protected by Copyright Law. Visual fine arts can be easily reproduced so that artists can make money selling prints, cards. limited editions, as well as the original work.

I wouldn't put all my online marketing efforts into selling artwork online but if you are an artist now, or if you have the urge to produce artwork, I have something to share with you. I found a company called

YOU CAN MAKE MORE MONEY

Fine Art America who will post your artwork and sell prints and cards for you free of charge. They make their money doing the printing and framing and customers have a wide variety of frames, colors, and papers, and mats that they can choose.

I think this is a great no cost opportunity for artists to showcase their work but I realize that selling artwork involves lots of promotion to gain a following, and this won't happen overnight or by itself, I suspect that just displaying artwork online will not be enough to make the cash register ring and that to be successful the site must be promoted to get people to visit the site on purpose and not by accident.

I am not saying that FineArtAmerica does not promote their artists. In fact they do an outstanding job of this and they promote artwork and images so they are searchable online. Nonetheless, if you expect to sell any amount of artwork you will want to advertise this yourself.

I am approaching my artwork as a fun retirement business now that I have some time to paint and I do not expect this to make a lot of money. However if over time my art business could eventually make a few hundred dollars a month, this would be worthwhile for me and fun at the same time.

ANOTHER GREAT OPPORTUNITY for ARTISTS AND DESIGNERS:

Artists and designers should be sure to visit the website by CafePress.com if you are interested in having your artwork printed and sold on a royalty basis. If you have a design that you think would sell if it was printed on T shirts, caps, bags, clothing, wallets, drinkware, posters, etc., then you can upload your design to CafePress and then select the products that you would like to sell. CafePress does the rest and will pay you a royalty on each item sold with no online shop to maintain, inventory to stock, or shipping hassles.

If you have a website, blog, or other built in audience, CafePress will allow you to set up an online shop with no Up Front Fees. When items with your designs are sold, you receive a royalty. CafePress will allow you to open as many shops as you like without putting a dime upfront. They have 2 ways to pay, either 10% of your royalties each month or as little as $5 per month.

Note that the real value of using FineArtAmerica or CafePress is that they can provide you with products to sell that are protected by copyright. You will have to advertise these products on your own so that people can see and buy your work.

5. VALUE ADDED BY ARTWORK:

Now I have mentioned the idea that most handmade items do not do well online and tried to present a realistic outlook for selling artwork online, I would like to suggest the idea of adding value to commercial items with your artwork.

If you want to make money online with your artwork this could be a great way to do it. For example you could buy some lampshades at discount prices and then paint images or designs on the lamp shade and mark up the price. The price can be increased because the lampshade is now unique. Although bulky, lampshades don't weigh much so the shipping cost should be low. By doing this you would have taken a common and faceless common household item and added value to it.

An example of adding value to a commercial item would be buying nice quality long sleeve T shirts and painting designs directly on the shirts. Another idea to add value would be to use your art to personalize good selling items by painting names on commercial items on a custom basis. This could be done on toys or children's furniture, or other gift items that are easy to ship.

CHOOSING YOUR FIRST PRODUCTS IDEAS:

Some people can get so bogged down looking for products to sell that they have a hard time making a choice. They are so worried about making a wrong choice that they never can get beyond this step.

The important thing is to find something that you think will sell and then give it a try. Unlike a marriage, you don't need to find the best possible choice. Anything that you think will make money will do. You'll find lots products and get lots of ideas as you begin to sell online.

If something works that's great. If it doesn't work out, then you can try something else. The product ideas that make money for you will naturally lead you to even better ideas. Everyone learns from failures and there will be some flops along the way. But the cost to try an idea is very low compared to other types of businesses, that this isn't even a real issue. Ideas by themselves are terrific but without your energy and action, they can never make money for you. This means that your energy and action is more important than the idea itself and is the main factor in your success.

You can sell
just about anything
if you try hard enough.

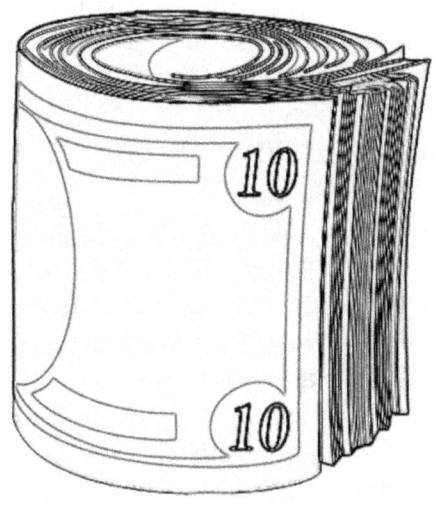

But if you really

want to make money,

sell something that

people want !

Chapter 5. The Business Side of Selling Online

Because you can start an online profit center for little more than the price of a cup of coffee, you might be tempted to begin right away by yourself without forming a company. This is OK but you will save a lot of money in taxes if you organize your business properly from day one.

EASTABLISH A LIMITED LIABILITY COMPANY:

Unless you already have an established business, I encourage you to formally organize your new business as a limited liability company, commonly called a LLC. You can do this by yourself in a few minutes over the telephone for less than $100.

A LLC combines the characteristics of a corporation and a partnership of sole proprietorship. Like a corporation a LLC limits liability of the owner but only requires a single owner. Like a partnership a LLC offers the availability of Pass Through Taxation and this is HUGE.

Once you have established your LLC then you can elect how you wish to be taxed. The best choice is for your LLC to be taxed as an S Corporation because the profit or loss from the LLC is passed through to its members.

If your LLC is not paying you wages then all the profit (or loss) would be posted on line 17 to your IRS Individual Income Tax Form 1040 and this amount would not be subjected to any self employment tax and would save you 15.3% in tax forever.

CAUTION:

If you fail to organize your business in this manner you will be penalized heavily. A self employed person without a LLC or an S Corp must pay self employment tax in addition to federal income tax. This consists of paying 12.4% of business profit for social security and 2.9% for medicare totaling 15.3% plus Federal and possibly State income tax as well.

If you pay yourself a wage from the LLC then these wages would be subject to payroll taxes but any profit beyond this amount would be completely exempt.

In addition there are a lot of other advantages and tax savings that are possible if you are organized in this manner so I highly suggest that you do this ASAP.

OPEN A CHECKING ACCOUNT FOR YOUR LLC.

You will want a separate checking account and a debit card linked to your LLC account.. This makes it much easier to prepare your taxes and it is required by the IRS. The debit card will allow you to make purchases online from the business account.

You won't need the notebook sized checkbook that the banks want to sell you. You can get by just fine with regular checks with carbonless copies. I really like the copy checks because you always have a copy of each check to simplify bookkeeping.

GET AN ACCOUNTING PROGRAM

You will need an accounting program for your computer to help you keep the books and prepare your taxes. You will need something more than a spreadsheet and should get an accounting program like QuickBooks which can generate a profit and loss statement and an income statement.

An LLC does require a little extra effort than filing as a self employed person but the tax savings are worth it. You will have to file for the LLC and also for yourself. By not having your checking account commingled with the business and by using a computer accounting program, tax preparation will be as easy as possible.

ESTABLISH A PAYPAL ACCOUNT:

You should open an account with PayPal.com for your business and be sure that it is linked to your business checking account. This will require an Employer ID number which you will get when you make the choice with the IRS so that you will be taxed as an S Corp.

Some customers use PayPal on a regular basis and use this to buy online. And you can use your PayPal account to buy merchandise by sending a eCheck from your PayPal account.

When you establish your PayPal account they will make a small deposit of a few cents into your account to make sure that everything is working properly. When you verify the amount of this deposit, your account is activated. When someone buys something from you and pays by PayPal you are notified about this by email. Then you have the option to return their money or transfer the balance into your checking account.

This takes about 4 business days and if you want

the money sooner you can transfer the balance to a PayPal debit card and use this right away. The fee for each PayPal transaction is a little over 3% and is similar to the discount fee that you would pay if you processed the credit card yourself. See details at PayPal.com.

BUSINESS TELEPHONE:

You may need to get a business telephone If you advertise your new business in print or the phone book. The phone company may insist that you pay for a business phone when they know that you are using the phone for business. But there is no reason to advertise your online business locally so this should not be a problem for you. If you did advertise your phone number locally you could avoid the high cost of a business phone by switching to a cell phone. Even though all your business related telephone expenses are deductible and there is no use in paying more than you have to for phone service.

SIGNS, LETTERHEAD, BUSINESS CARDS:

Signs and cards are not needed to run an online business since you are not looking for local customers.

OFFICE EXPENSE:

You won't need an office but it is nice to have a dedicated work area. Do not make the mistake of trying to take your home office as a business expense on your taxes since this is an audit trigger. You can, however, deduct the cost of the heat and electricity for your home office and work area.

REGISTER YOUR LLC WITH YOUR STATE'S SECRETARY OF STATE:

You will have to register your LLC or Corporation with your State's Secretary of State every year. This can be done online and lets people know who is doing business in their State. There is no cost as long as you file the registration on time.

LOCAL BUSINESS PERMITS +REGISTRATION:

Some areas require you to register your business locally and possibly get some kind of permit. Your City Hall can advise.

SALES TAX:

If you live in a State that has a Sales Tax, you will have to pay this for all in-State sales whether you collect the tax or not. You will probably be operating on a small margin, you might as well add and collect the tax, since people are used to paying this anyway. Either way, you will have to pay this.

INTERNET SALES TAX:

It looks like a new internet sales tax might become law at some point. This will most likely have a large cutoff, say one million dollars a year. So anyone selling less than this amount will be exempt from personally paying this although this does impact smaller sellers who sell through Amazon, eBay, etc. since these businesses must pay the tax.

Taking these steps to establish your new business and bank account before you begin will allow you to take the maximum tax advantage and keep you from co-mingling your personal money with your business account.

If you don't formally organize right away it isn't the end of the world, but bookkeeping and taxes preparation will be easier, and your taxes will be lower, if you do this before you start selling online.

Once you are organized as a Corporation, you'll get a sense of pride and accomplishment right away knowing that you are more than the man on the street, you are the President of a Corporation, your Corporation.

One nice aspect of being organized as a "LLC" or "S Corp" is that people think that you are Real and not some part timer doing business out of their garage. They do not know how large or small your business is. All they know for sure is that they are doing business with a business and not an individual. And because of this people like to think that if they need more product or assistance in the future, that you will be there for them.

Making your own
web pages and websites
is a lot easier than
you might think.

YOU CAN DO THIS!

Chapter 6. How to Make an Online Profit Center

Once you have decided which products you wish to sell, you will want to give some thought about building profit center websites. Note that if you only plan to market on other websites like eBay, Amazon, Etsy, Craigslist, etc. you won't need your own website right away.

But the cost is so low and the benefits can be so great you'll want to start building website profit centers for the products you test that prove worthwhile. This can be done without much computer experience at all, thanks to the software that most low cost web hosts offer today. The cost to build and maintain your own site can be less per month than most people spend on coffee in a day.

You won't need a big site with lots of space. A basic e-commerce sight with your own domain, email, and shopping cart. is about all you need. The low cost web hosts listed later in this chapter can have your website online in just a few days from the time you sign up.

New domains take a few days to propagate so that they can be accessed using the domain name. Then you can start putting your site together and testing it to be sure everything on the site works as it should.

YOU CAN BUY AN ESTABLISHED WEBSITE:

It is possible to buy an established website that is producing a monthly income for a few thousand dollars or less. If you can find a website that you like that is already making money this may be a great way to get your feet wet. See the websites that feature lists of established websites for sale in the resource section at the end of this book.

WEBSITE OPTIONS and STRATEGIES:

There are a variety of low cost ways to build your own websites and web pages. The cost to build and maintain a web site can be as low as $2 a month, or $25 - $50 or more and these sites can be built with little or no experience using the host's software and control panel.

One approach is to build one website and place everything you wish to sell on that one website. This makes it easy to showcase all the items you wish to sell in one location. If your product line has a theme like music, sporting goods, sewing, etc. then using one website might make sense.

But if you are selling unrelated items then it may make more sense to have several websites, each devoted to one item or groups of similar items. Because you can set up and maintain a web site for as little as few dollars a month, cost is not an issue. By doing this each website can have its own domain so people can remember it easily.

For example if your website has a domain name like JoesPetSupplies.com that showcased all the pet products you wished to sell, you might have a page with dog beds, another page for dog toys, another for cat toys, cat beds, etc. The URL (web address) for these pages would have an extension on the address so it would now read JoesPetSupplies.com/dogtoy.html and this would be the page featuring dogtoys. When someone clicked on a toy that they liked a new page would come up with a URL like JoesPetSupplies.com/dogfrisbee201/html .

All of these pages are different and have a different URL. Eventually a large commerce site with 40 items might have 50 web pages or more, each with its own URL and as you can see these can easily get long and awkward to remember.

Another thing to consider when choosing a domain name is how it will look in print. Like emails, web domains are not case sensitive. This means that although the words in the domain are run together without spaces, capital letters may be used to make the domain name easier to read and easier to remember.

For example this domain name below is hard to read: americantrucksandtrailers.com but if capitals letters are used in the domain this is easier to read: AmericanTrucksAndTrailers.com and it is also easier to remember.

AN EVEN BETTER APPROACH:

Another approach that works well is to build and maintain a separate website for each profit center item or small group of items that you wish to sell. As mentioned the cost can be very low, only a few dollars a month for each website / product group that you wish to sell.

This means that you can have a different domain for each website that you have and the name of the domain can be related to the product you wish to sell. Instead of a URL like JoesPetSupplies.com/dogfrisbee201/html your domain could be named something like LowPricedFrisbees.com and the title of the site could be "Frisbees for Dogs, low prices and great selection."

Both the domain and the site's title make it more likely that someone looking for a Frisbee for their dog will find you using search engines.

YOUR WEBSITE WILL NEED SEVERAL PAGES:

The simplest ecommerce website could be only one page to both advertise and sell a product. But this would be a waste. Once you own a domain and pay for hosting, it doesn't cost any more to have additional pages built into your website.

You will always need the home page (and regardless of its title the file name for this must always be index.html). You will want additional pages so that you can detail each product you wish to sell.

It is a good idea to have a page or two to inspire consumer trust by making the website something more than a one page online flyer. Most websites will have a page titled "About" which describes the company and management. Many websites will have a page titled "Policy" that describes when items are shipped and how or if they can be returned.

Two other pages are often used by webmasters. One is the "Thank You" page. This would be the page that the customer would see after they successfully completed a purchase when using your shopping cart or PayPal buttons.

Note, a PayPal button is a button that you can put

on your website and use instead of a shopping cart to purchase a product. These are linked to PayPal and are coded with your price and product info and work like a shopping cart for individual items.

One other page that you might want within your website is a "Sorry but your order did not go through" page. This is the page that they would see if for some reason the customer did not continue with the purchase.

POSTING A TELEPHONE NUMBER ON THE SITE:

If you are operating regular hours and would like to deal with customers by phone in real time, then you will want to post your telephone number on the website.

Many ecommerce websites do not post a telephone number for customers to contact because nobody is home to answer the phone. Also most online sellers have a take it or leave it attitude and they know that they will not lose many sales because of this. Nowadays people are used to shopping online and do not need human contact to assist them.

Some customers shop online but they only buy over the telephone. Some are reluctant to provide credit card info online and others have specific shipping instructions or other concerns not easily addressed online. Most online sellers are not equipped to take credit card info over the phone and you will want to be able to do this if you deal with customers by phone. PayPal can help with this.

PAYPAL DEBIT CARD:

If you have a PayPal account you may wish to get a free PayPal debit card. Normally when people send you money through PayPal, and you transfer the balance, it takes 3 – 4 business days before the money is available in your account. If you have a PayPal account, you can transfer the balance to your PayPal debit card and use this money right away.

EMAIL ADDRESSES FOR YOUR WEBSITES:

Most people choose to use an email address from their domain on their website. Often this is sales at XYZ.com or info at XYZ.com. When someone sends an email to an address like this, it is then forwarded to another email. This is the best way to handle this but it has some drawbacks that you should know about.

If you have more than one website and each has a different email address you will have to add these to your PayPal account. Unless you set up different accounts in your email program for each address, any questions that you answered or replies that you sent would show that they were from your personal email address.

This means that when you reply to the customer, they won't know that it is from your website until they open the email unless this is made clear in the subject line. For example if the email came from JoeBlow at Verizon.net and the subject line read, "Order Status #12345786", the customer would not know what the email was really about until they opened it. But if the subject line read, "Joes Sunglasses, order shipped", then the personal email address that is used is less confusing.

WEB PAGE SIZE:

You can make a web page any size that you like. Since so many people use large computer monitors with high resolution, it can be tempting to build a web page that is wider than it is tall. This is perfectly fine if everyone who views your site has a new computer with a large monitor but this will not be the case.

If you build a web page that is too wide people with older computers will not be able to see the whole page without scrolling to the right. People with smart phones will have your 1600 pixel wide web page crammed into a 2.5 inch display. Also a wide web page will not print well and this can be frustrating for users.

Ideally a user would not have to scroll at all to see the entire page so it is important to place everything you want people to see in the top and middle of a page as opposed to the bottom.

There are no standard sizes but I like to build web pages that are 700 – 1000 pixels wide by about 800 high.

KISS (Keep it Simple Stupid):

The longer I live, the better advice this turns out to be. There is no reason to impress people who visit your web site with Hollywood style graphics and web tricks that dazzle the user.

Ecommerce websites are about selling things and nothing more. They should inform, inspire, and be easy to navigate. The site name should be easy to spell and easy to remember. These sites should download quickly without sacrificing anything needed to sell the product. If you need several pictures, use them. If a video is required, use it. Just don't waste your time creating a logo that rivals the MGM Lion because it will not lead to increased sales.

USING AN OLD MAIL ORDER TECHNIQUE TO ENHANCE ONLINE SALES:

A few years ago lots of people were attracted to the idea of mail order sales and finding money in their mail box. One strategy that was promoted was to find a product that you could sell via classified ads in newspapers.

Once you had the product then the idea was to experiment with different classified ads until you found just the right ad copy that would create enough sales to pay for the ad and make a small profit.

Then if you wanted to make more money, you would place additional ads in more and more newspapers as your budget allowed. So if an ad made an average profit of $50, then ten ads in ten different papers could be expected to make about $500 in profit and this idea could easily be expanded beyond this.

The reason that I mention this now is that this idea can work even better today. A small classified ad, like "Really Cool dog frisbees at the lowest prices. See at LowPricedFrisbees.com" would not cost much to run in the local want ads. In fact the profit from one or two sales would likely pay for the ad.

The URL in an ad like this is easy to read and easy to remember but a domain name like JoesPetSupplies.com/dogfrisbee201.html is another story.

In any case if you find a classified ad that directs people to your website and generates enough sales to make a consistent profit, then you have a money maker on your hands. The more ads you place, the more product you will sell.

WEB SITE TITLE:

The first thing to consider is the title of the site. This is important because a good title will help you rank better in the search engines so more people are likely to find you. Try some searches on your own for competitive products to help you get a good title idea. A site title like, "Betty's Favorite Kitchen Things" would be a poor choice compared to "Kitchen Utensils, Tools, and Gadgets".

WEBSITE DOMAIN:

The domain (also called a URL) is the name of the web site for example ChoiceKitchenUtensils.com. There are other extensions like .org, .us, .biz but you will want a website that ends in .com because this is what most shoppers are used to.

You should be sure that your web domain name is easy to spell or you will lose potential customers who are trying to find you.

Most website hosting companies will offer a free domain for the first year and they will have a domain checker for use to see if a domain is available or already taken. No two domains can be exactly the same. Generally it will cost about $15 per year to keep your domain active and sometimes this is included in the hosting package.

YOU CAN MAKE MORE MONEY

WEBSITE HOSTING:

Once you own a domain you need to have your web files stored on a server so that people can see your site. The companies that do this are called website hosting companies.

If you build your own website (more on this later) then the cost can be $2 a month or less. Imagine renting a storefront and keeping it open 24 hours a day for only 50¢ a week. It's amazingly affordable. This opportunity wasn't here yesterday, and it might not be here tomorrow, but it is here now. Today we can operate our own websites for just a fraction of what this cost even a few years ago.

LOW COST WEB HOSTING OPTIONS:
Today we are lucky because it is easy and inexpensive to design and host your own website. Just a few years ago people had to hire web developers or learn to do this for themselves. It often cost thousands of dollars to build a website and a large monthly fee to host it. But now there are many ways to build and host an e commerce website without knowing much about html or computer code.

This is because most low cost web hosting companies also offer free website builder software that makes it easy to build a website. They have templates you can download and then you can edit the template by replacing the pictures and text within the frames of the template. These sites offer a variety of PHP scripts including Blogs and Shopping Carts. They also offer video tutorials to help you get started and customer support.

It may take a few days to build your first site by

yourself using this kind of software but once you see how this works, you'll probably think that it is fun. Unlike print ads, websites are dynamic and can always be easily updated.

Here are a few low cost web hosting companies to take a look at. Each offers several different hosting plans. Be sure to get a plan that supports e-commerce, offers a free web builder, free domain name, and a control panel. I'm sure that you can find other good companies as well.

1dollar-webhosting.com	iPage.com
Justhost.com	Bluehost.com
Fatcow.com	Hostmonster.com
Volusion.com	Web.com

Note that Volusion isn't the lowest cost web host but they do offer a lot of nice services and support. They specialize in e commerce websites and they claim that their websites sell 300% more than other e-commerce websites.

BUILDING WEBSITES WITH WYSIWYG EDITORS:

In addition to the free web building software provided by most hosting companies, you may want to purchase a WYSIWYG, *What You See Is What You Get,* html editor, for your computer. These types of web page editors allow you to have greater control about how a web page looks and feels. In all fairness they do have a steep learning curve so most online sellers will not chose to go this route. It's not that it is complicated, it is

69

that it is unfamiliar.

With these WYSIWYG editors you usually begin with a blank page. Then you divide the page into custom frames and fill in the frames with text and or images. Because you design the frames yourself you get much better control about the positioning of your content.

Web pages aren't like printed pages made with desktop publishing software that can control elements on the page to the thousands of an inch. Web pages normally don't print well either but this is not my point. Because of different computer resolutions setting, operating systems, browsers, and browser settings it is possible to have 5 different computers sitting next to each other showing the same web page and have none of the web pages look the same.

If the web page uses text on the page, this can be badly distorted if the user has the text view option set at over 100%. In extreme cases it can make the web page unreadable.

Web designers learn this right away and have several ways to deal with this problem. One way to handle this is to not use text at all but use pictures with text instead. However when this is done, none of the pictures of the text are searchable by the search engines.

Once you have a page made with one of these editors you can preview how the page looks in various web browsers and fix anything that doesn't look right.

Normally you will keep all the files for a web site in the same folder on your computer. The home page must have a file name of index.html but it could have any title that you wished. Other pages could be named anything you like as long as they had the .html extension. All the pictures and other pages used in the website would also be stored in the same folder.

Next you would load all the files up using FTP software or the host's control panel. Then you would normally view each page of the site carefully and test all links and behaviors online to be sure that they all worked properly. If you installed a shopping cart this must be tested as well.

Sometimes when you are trying to look at your latest version of a web page online, it will not display the new version of the page on your browser. If this happens you will have to reload the page under the view menu of the web browser to see the new page.

If this still does not display the new page, wait an hour or so and try to bring up the page again. Sometimes files get loaded up instantly and other times there can be a slight delay before the new page can be seen.

WEBSITES BUILT WITH FRAMES:

Lots of website are built with custom frames. Basically this is a way to divide the page into little boxes (or frames) and a, graphic, picture, or text can be placed in each box.

Frames gives the web page designer a lot of control in how the page looks and makes the page easy to edit. Most of the template web designs that hosting companies offer are made using frames. Take a peek a few pages ahead and notice the diagram labeled step 1.

This is an example of how a basic web page made with frames looks when it is naked and without content. Notice that in this case there is a space for a large picture across the top and a space for another on the left hand side.

The right hand lower corner has a table inserted

in it and this is three columns wide and four rows high. This is where the product photo is placed and beneath it the product name, price and stock number. Because these are placed in a table within the frame it is easy to substitute new product photos, prices, and stock numbers without disturbing other elements on the page. Below the 3x4 table you will see two boxes where text will be inserted.

The next illustration, step 2, shows how the page looks when using the WYSIWYG editor with the top picture placed in the box at the top of the page.

The step 3 illustration shows how the page would look in the html editor after all the pictures and text were placed on the page. Finally, the step 4. Illustration shows how the page will look online when seen with a web browser. All the frame lines can no longer be seen and the elements on the page are held in position by the hidden frames and table.

Obviously this is not a course in building websites and web pages but I wanted to give you an idea about how web pages are made. If you see a web page that you like and save it, you can open this file with a WYSIWYG editor and see how that web page is constructed.

There is something I haven't mentioned about the step 4 stage website illustration. Even though the caption says that the page is completed, it really isn't. There are two things left to do before this page is ready to be uploaded and put online. The text and other links have to be added and the meta tag info like the title, description, and keywords must be included or search engines will not be able to find the page.

step 1. create frames

step2. add pictures and text

step 3. pictures added + links inserted

step 4. basic web page completed

IMAGE MAPPING:

     Besides building web pages with frames and then filling each framed box with content as in the previous example, there is another popular way to build a web page using image mapping.

     Imagine that the step 4 web page example you just viewed was made from one large image 800 pixels wide and 600 pixels high. All the text seen on the page would not really be text but a picture of the text instead. A web page like this would use image mapping to define hidden hot spots and links on the page. See below. Each hidden boxed area would be linked to bring up a different web page. The contact link would either bring up a page describing ways to contact the website or it would be linked to bring up a pre-addressed email window.

I should mention once again that any web page that uses text can be badly distorted and rendered almost unreadable if the user has chosen to enlarge the text in their browser. Some users with poor vision choose to enlarge the text as much as 300%. If this happens some text will overlap other text or push it down the page. The position of the pictures on the page can be moved down the page as well.

The best way to avoid this is to use one large image for the website and use image mapping to insert links and behaviors. If you do this, it will not matter what view options users choose to use on their computers because this cannot distort the page. Everyone will see your page exactly as you do.

If you will be changing products of pictures on your website, then you will want you use frames and tables since this makes editing the page a little easier.

POSTING TEXT ADS USING HTML:

If you are going to be selling on eBay or other websites you will want to learn a little about html. This is the language of world wide web.

If you didn't post in html your listing would be plain text. All the text would be the same color, font, and size. No bolding, centering, or linking would be possible without html.

But if you posted your web ad using html all this would be possible. Your ad will really stand out from the other ads that are plain text. You can do this easily with a free online editor at 4html.net/Online-text-to-HTML-converter-831.html

Chapter 7. Image & Photo Editing

Since you will be using pictures of the products that you wish to sell, you will need to know some basics about editing images. Adobe Photoshop™ is the industry leader in image editing software but the learning curve is steep. The full program costs about $600 and they offer the lite version, Photoshop Elements™ for about $100.

I did find a very good online photo editor that is quite powerful, easy to use, and free of charge. See at Pixlr.com .

Most products will already have pictures that you can use and will require little editing other than cropping, resizing, etc. If you intend to take your own pictures then much more editing will be required. In addition image editor programs are also used to build graphic elements that are used on web pages.

One thing to know about graphic images, and photos to be used on the web, is that computer screens show a 72 dpi (dot per inch) image so there is no sense using a resolution higher than this since it increases file size and needlessly slows download time. On a computer screen, a high resolution image will not display any better than a low resolution image. Although this is not as much of a problem as it used to be, some users with slow connections will not wait long to download a page and could get tired of waiting for a page to load and decide to go elsewhere.

This chapter is intended only to introduce you to some of the more useful tools and features found in today's image editors like Adobe Photoshop Elements™ . Some of the commands discussed here may be found under menus with different names , so you may have to look within the program that you are using because these menus might not be quite the same but the tools and commands should be similar.

To open a graphic image or photo choose the Open Command under the File Menu and navigate to the file. If the Tool menu is not showing go to the Window Menu, and be sure that Tools is checked so that you can use the Tools if you need them.

Like word processors, it is important to understand that any changes that you make to an image will not be permanent until the file is SAVED.

IMAGE MENU:

MODE:

In the Image Menu if you click on MODE you will see the mode of the image that you have opened. It will probably be RGB, CMYK, Indexed Color, Lab Color, etc. You can change the color mode if you like and also will have the option to choose Grayscale if you wish . Note that Grayscale is different than Black and White and if this is what you want, the B&W mode change option can be found under Adjustments on the image Menu.

ADJUSTMENTS:

One of the most used adjustments is the BIGHTNESSS / CONTRAST adjustment. If you click on this a window with slider controls will appear. Be sure that the preview box is checked and then experiment with different settings. If you are happy with the change SAVE the file with a different file name so that you always retain the original image if needed.

YOU CAN MAKE MORE MONEY

Another very useful TOOL found under Adjustments in the Image Menu is the **LEVELS CONTROL**. This allows more control in making the image darker or lighter than just using the Brightness / Contrast control. Once again be sure that the preview window is checked and experiment with the 3 slide controls which look like arrow heads.

There are some other useful options that you will want to try that are found under Adjustments like **HUE/ SATURATION, COLOR BALANCE, and REPLACE COLOR** to name a few. This is the fun part about Image Editors, you can adjust and play with photos and graphics to get them just the way that you want them.

IMAGE SIZE is a menu choice that you will use all the time and this is found in the Image Menu. When you click on this a box will appear on the screen showing the width and height of the image in pixels (or inches, cm, mm, picas). The box will also show the resolution. Also notice that there are three boxes in the lower corner and these should all be checked, scale styles, constrain proportions, and resample image.

To change the resolution of the image, for example, just enter a new number in the box and click OK. To change the image size, change the height or the width and click OK. If the constrain proportion box was checked, the height / width ratio of the picture would be unchanged.

The **CANVAS SIZE** option is also found under the Image Menu and this is a little different than just changing the image size. It is usually used to add more space to an image's document or paper size without changing the size of the image itself. For example you might want a few more inches of white space on the top or the bottom of the image so that you had room to add text to the picture.

The **IMAGE ROTATION** choice applies to the entire picture. This can be rotated by degree to presets like 90, 180 degrees clockwise or counter clockwise, or the rotation can be arbitrary. Note that this applies to the entire image. If you wanted to rotate only a portion of the image, this would be done by selecting the portion you wished to rotate and then using the Transform option found under the Edit menu.

THE EDIT MENU:

The **UNDO / STEP BACKWARDS** menu options are a lifesaver because, with these, you never have to worry about messing up your work. Most Image Editors have at least one level of UNDO and most have more. This lets you try different ideas, and if you don't like them, return to the way the photo was before you changed it. Think of UNDO as a step backward control.

The **CUT / PASTE** commands work much like a word processor. If working in Layers, Flatten the image first, and then select an area of the picture to be CUT. Then you could PASTE this into another photo. Note that both the original image and the new image must share the same resolution or the Pasted image will be distorted.

The **FILL** command opens a dialog box and gives you the choice of painting the selected area with either the Background color or the Foreground color. You will have a choice between a normal fill mode and a variety of other choices. Also the opacity of the fill can be chosen as a percentage.

The **STROKE** command brings up a dialog box where you can specify details about stroking the selected area. This can be specified in width by pixels, by color, and by location, and mode. This is often used to picture frame a selected area and can be placed on the inside, center, or outside of a selection. Opacity can be specified here as well.

The **TRANSFORM / FREE TRANSFORM** option apply to a selected area and are used to skew, scale, distort, rotate, and flip the selection. Usually when you make this choice the selected area will be shown with little boxes, or handles. By moving these individually the image is changed. Before the program will allow you to do anything else, you must either accept the transformation or abandon the change.

THE SELECT MENU:

Sometimes the **SELECT** command will be in the Edit menu but usually this has a menu of its own. Before you can apply a command or operation to a picture, you must first select it under the SELECT MENU. These programs are very powerful and basically need to know exactly what picture (or file) you are specifying and what you want to do to it.

The **DESELECT** command does exactly what you think. If something is selected, it will unselect it so that you can select something else to apply another operation.

The **INVERSE** command selects everything except the selected area. This is very useful when editing photos. For example lets say that you have a photo of a person standing in front of a solid blue background, and you wanted to cut the person out and paste them in another photo. By SELECTING the blue background, and then INVERTING it, you have now selected the more complicated image of the person. Then you could COPY this and paste the person into another photo.

THE FILTER MENU:

Most Image Editors will have some fun and useful filters to play with. These can change a photo into various artistic styles, like charcoal or pen and ink. There are way to many to talk about here but I know that you will have fun trying them out when you get time. There is something cool about making a picture of a Rose look as if it has been chrome plated or turned into stained glass.

The **SHARPEN** filters are the most useful to know about for online sellers. There are a few Sharpen Options that you can try but the one I want you to know about is called **UNSHARP MASK**. This is derived from a darkroom technique used to sharpen images. I swear by this option and think that you will be really happy with it too. When the dialog box appears you check the preview box and experiment with the three slider type controls. I almost always choose an Amount of 50% and a Radius of 2 pixels with the Threshold set at zero. This should be done only once or the photo will degrade. Try it and see how well this works for you.

YOU CAN MAKE MORE MONEY

THE LAYER MENU:

Using Layers can be confusing at first but once you get used to this, I think that you'll really like it. The original Layer is the beginning photo and then other Layers can be stacked over this. Think of the Layers as clear sheets that overlay the original image. They are numbered and can re-arranged. They can even be made invisible or they can be all melded together. When all the Layers are made into one Layer, the image is said to be flattened.

The Layers are useful because they let you change and experiment with different ideas, colors, layouts, etc and can be easily edited. For example, if text was added to a photo, this would be in a different Layer so the position, wording, fonts, and colors could be moved at will and changed anytime. Once you get comfortable using Layers they are great. But if they are cumbersome for you, just keep Flattening the image so you are only working in one Layer.

When you choose **NEW** under the Layer menu then you are given the option to add another Layer to your work.

The **RASTERIZE** command found in the Layer menu is extremely important when you work with text in an image editor program. Image editors are not very good at handling text, especially smaller sizes at low resolutions. Remember this is because it is producing a picture of the text and not text itself. So when adding text to an image, it is important to Rasterize the type before you save the image. You can Rasterize each layer individually or do this all at once.

The **ARRANGE** command gives you the option to change the order that the Layers are stacked so that you can move a Layer from the front to the back or visa versa.

FLATTEN IMAGE is the command used to merge all visible Layers into one. This is required to save an image file with Layers as a .JPG image, the most widely used image file format.

OTHER MENUS:

The other menus like **FILE, VIEW, and WINDOW** shouldn't give you much trouble since these are often found in other programs.

COMMON IMAGE EDITING TOOLS:

Most Image Editor programs work in a similar manner and have similar menus and similar tools. The TOOLS appear in the Tool Bar and this is in a separate floating window than the picture or image that you are working on. The Tool Bar appears when Tools are checked in the Window Menu.

The arrow shaped tool is called the **MOVE TOOL**. This is used to move a selected object or to move the handles that appear around a selection when using a transform command like scale or rotate. To use the MOVE TOOL, first select a portion of the image using the selection tools described below. Next click on the MOVE

TOOL, and drag the selection where you want it by clicking on the selection, and with the mouse button still held down, drag the selection where you wish and release the mouse button.

The **RECTANGLE SELECTION TOOL** is shaped like a dotted rectangle. When this is selected you can select a rectangular part of a photo. To select an area click the top left hand corner of the part you want selected and drag the cursor down and to the right to make the selection. Once this is done, the selection can be copied or cut. It can be resized, or skewed. The color can be altered, or the area could be filled with textures or images. Any number of adjustments, filters, or effects can be preformed once an area is selected.

The **OVAL SELECTION TOOL** is often hidden under the Rectangular Selection Tool. When a Tool has a little tiny triangle in the lower right hand corner of the Tool Icon this means that there are other Tools available and you only see the one that is selected. Click on the arrow and you will see the other TOOLS that are available.
Note: If you want to select a perfect circle or square, choose the appropriate tool and hold the shift key down as you drag down and across the selection.

The **LASSO SELECTION TOOL** has an icon like a lariat with a little handle at the bottom. This tool allows you to draw a loop around an object to select it. As long as the mouse button is held down as the cursor is moved around an object, it continues to follow the path but if the path is not completed when the mouse button is released, the Lasso finishes the loop with a straight line back to the starting point.

The **MAGNETIC LASSO SELECTION TOOL** is even more fun and found in the Lasso sub-menu. Just draw a path closely around an object and the path closes and clings to the objects perimeter as if it was magnetic!

The **MAGIC WAND SELECTOR TOOL** is really wonderful and works best with solid colors or gradients without much contrast. The icon for the tool looks a little like a sparkler. When this is selected and then clicked in an area of a photo, it makes the selection using color. This range of color and sensitivity can be adjusted by inserting a number into the tolerance window between 1 and 100. 1 is the least sensitive and 100 is the most sensitive setting. If you experiment with the tolerance settings, I am sure that you will find this a time saving tool for many situations.

The **CROP TOOL** is used to reduce the some of the waste (or extra space) in a picture while retaining the meat (or subject). The Crop Tool has an icon that looks like two carpenters squares. For example if you had a picture of a friend at the beach, you might want to eliminate most of the people around your friend so that the predominant subject of the photo was your friend. The sunbathers around your friend would be cut and removed from the top bottom and side of the original photo leaving only (or mostly) the picture of your friend.

The **EYEDROPPER TOOL** looks like an eye dropper as you might expect. When it is selected and you click on a portion of a photo, the EYEDROPPER

86

selects the exact color that is shown where the EYEDROPPER was clicked. This color shows in the color foreground window of the Tool Bar until another color is selected.

The **SPOT HEALING BRUSH** is a fun Tool used to retouch photographs and its icon looks a little like an eraser on a pencil. Try this on a close up of a person's face. Look around their face until you see a blemish or discoloration. By clicking once over the blemish with the Spot Healing Brush, the blemish will be gone.

The **BRUSH TOOLS / PENCIL TOOLS** have icons that looks like a little paint brush or pencil. It is used like a paint brush and it has a ton of options. Besides choosing the size of the brush in pixels, you can choose among various types of brushes and brush tips as well. You can control the hardness of the brush and operate in many modes besides normal like color burn, overlay or difference. The opacity and flow can be changed from 1% - 100% and it can be made to act like an air brush instead of a normal paint brush. When the Brush Tool is selected it paints the color that is shown in the foreground window of the Tool Bar.
The **PENCIL TOOL** works much like the brush tool and is useful for drawing lines or repairing images at the pixel level/

The **CLONE STAMP TOOL** is another fun and useful tool to know about. Its icon looks like a rubber stamp. It is used to copy complex patterns and portions of pictures and then paint these either somewhere else on the image or to another image entirely. Like the Brush Tool you click on the CLONE STAMP and select the size of the brush. Next you place the brush over the area that you wish to copy and press the Option (or Alt) key down as you click the mouse and this selects the target area to be copied. Next move the cursor to another part of the picture and press and drag the cursor to the right. This will paint the target image in the new location. The target can be made to follow the cursor as you paint or always remain stationary.

The **ERASER TOOL** looks like a little eraser and acts accordingly. When selected and the mouse button is held down and moved across the picture it will erase a path by painting the background color.

The **BLUR, SHARPEN, and SMUDGE TOOLS** are located in the same sub menu and are used to fine tune and touch up photos. The icon for the BLUR TOOL looks like a drop of water. When selected and a brush size is chosen, this will smooth over and eliminate the jagged edges of an image. Keep the mouse button pushed down and go back and forth across the jagged edge until you are happy with the results.
The **SHARPEN TOOL** icon looks like a triangle. When worked across the edge of an image of a person's face for example, this will sharpen the edge.
The **SMUDGE TOOL** icon looks like a pointed finger and is used to smudge a spot on an image instead of blurring it or sharpening it.

The **BURN, DODGE, and SPONGE TOOLS** are used to touch up photographs. The BURN TOOL has an icon that looks like a hand with closed fingers. When selected the cursor is placed over a place on an image, and when clicked, that spot on the image is made Darker.

The **DODGE TOOL** icon is shaped like a small magnifying glass and lightens the image instead of darkening it.

The **SPONGE TOOL** icon looks like a wet sponge and acts accordingly when used over part of a photo.

There are other Tools that you will discover but I have covered the ones that you would use the most except for the TEXT TOOL and the MAGNIFYING GLASS.

The **TEXT TOOL** icon is a capital T and used to insert Text into an image. When this is selected and clicked into an image a NEW LAYER is created. Like word processors you can select the font, size, color, and style of the text you wish to insert. Also like word processors the justification can be selected. A click of the mouse with the TEXT TOOL selected will produce a flashing line as an insert point. Just type in (or paste) the text you wish to use. By using the MOVE Tool the text can be moved and placed anywhere on the image you like. When you are happy with this, be sure to go to the LAYER MENU and select RASTERIZE Type. Once you Rasterize the type it cannot be changed or edited although the Layer (and type) can be moved until the image is Flattened.

The **MAGNIFYING GLASS** icon is usually at the bottom of the Tool Bar and looks more like a magnifying glass than the Dodge Tool icon. It is used to enlarge the picture and this happens every time the mouse is clicked when the magnifying glass is selected until the image is enlarged to the pixel level. At this high level magnification images can be repaired pixel by pixel if need be. The magnification level is usually expressed as a percentage and if viewing an image at the pixel level this magnification could be as high as 3200%. To reduce the magnification select the magnifying glass, place the cursor over the image, hold down the option (Alt) key and click the mouse. Each click will reduce the size until you reach a magnification level that you are happy with.

The **FOREGROUND / BACKGROUND** Tool Bar Windows are located at the bottom of the Tool Bar and show you which colors are current foreground and background selections. To choose a new foreground color for example double click on the foreground color and a color picker is displayed that will allow you to chose a new color. When you click OK the new color is displayed in the foreground window. To make this the Background color, click on the double arrow found near these windows. When you do the foreground color becomes the background color choice and visa versa.

WORKING WITH PRODUCT PICTURES:

Most image editors work like Adobe Photoshop™ and use some of the same tools and icons that are listed here. You will probably want to take the tutorials available for your image editor and I encourage you to get an after market manual if one is available for your program. It won't take long to learn the basics but these programs are so powerful they take a long time to truly master.

To begin you would open a picture using the file menu. Then you could view the image size under the image menu and see the size of the image in pixels. Then if you want to change the image size, be sure that the constrain proportions option is checked and enter the desired height or width in pixels, and click OK.

The other pixel number for height or width will change, so that the picture will have the same aspect ratio as before. Only the image size will have changed. If you fail to check the constrain proportions box in the image size window, then your image will be distorted and not retain its original height and width ratio.

Once your image is resized then you may wish to adjust the brightness, levels, contrast, color, sharpness, etc. To do this first select the entire image by choosing select all, and then experiment with different filters. If you have the preview box checked you will be able to see the effect of the filter as you are adjusting it. If you don't want to save any adjustments just hit cancel.

If you use the sharpen filter be careful not to overdo it. I like the Unsharp Mask filter set at 50% and 2 pixels wide and a zero threshold. I like this method of sharpening a lot better than the Sharpen Tool found in the Tool Bar and hope that you'll try it too.

Even if the picture that you wish to use looks pretty good you may wish to adjust the brightness, contrast, color balance, or sharpness. You may also wish to add text to the picture showing the price, the name of your website, or to list special features.

Your images should be saved in .jpg or .jpeg format with file names that mean something to you. For example a file name of DSC1025686.jpg doesn't really help you if you have to locate this later but a file name like modeltrain201.jpg would be a much better choice.

As mentioned these programs are quite powerful and have a lot of tools and options. For example if you choose the brush tool you can change the size, type, hardness, and shape of the brush. You can choose a color and paint at 100% opacity or a lesser value. You can select up to twenty brush modes besides normal, like color, darken, lighten, dissolve burn, hue, etc. and these settings determines how the brush works. The more you use these programs the more you will like them.

One of the nicest features of most image editing programs is that they can step backwards and have several layers of Undo in case you make a mistake and wish to step backward. Obviously if you have made the image worse you can close the image without saving it and start over.

One of the most frustrating things about modern image editors for new users is learning to use Layers. Once you get used to working with Layers. The Layers are great because they allow you to really experiment by adding images, elements, and text so that each can be edited, moved within the image, resized, hidden, etc. until you get the image just the way you want it. If you find working with Layers confusing, be sure the image that you are working on is only one layer by choosing Flatten Image.

USING TEXT IN AN IMAGE FILE:

When you add text to an image the program creates a New Layer. Image editors don't handle text very well especially in the smaller font sizes and with low resolution (72 dpi) images. To place text in an image choose the text icon and click it in your image. Then check the font, size, and color options that you want and begin typing.

When you get this about the way you want it you can use the Move Tool in the tool menu to move the text exactly where you want it. By clicking back to the text

92

icon and highlighting the text you can still change the font, size, color, etc. Once you are happy with this, then Rasterize the text using the Rasterize command found in the Layer Menu. This makes the text print much better and then choose Flatten Image from the Layer Menu.

It is a good idea to Save this image using another file name so that you still have the original untouched image if you need this later.

It is important to understand the difference between a text file and an image file. Text files are small in size. The text can be edited by changing the words, fonts, sizes, colors, and alignment. Once the text has been Rasterized it can no longer be edited.

I could write a small paragraph and save it as a text file. Or I could take a picture of the text and save this as an image file. If you looked at the two files side by side on your computer they would look exactly the same. But the image file of the text would have a much larger file size. It would take a lot of effort to change the wording or anything about the image file. The image file could not be spell checked because it is a picture of the text and not the text itself.

This is important to understand because internet search engines scan web pages looking for keywords and phrases. An image file of text cannot be indexed by the search engines so the content of the image of the paragraph used in this example is not searchable.

Most product photos will be relatively small in size and you might wish to work with an image like this while viewing it at over 100%. This is fine but always preview your image at the 100% size before you save it.

This chapter is not intended to be a course about using photo editors but instead a few tips about working with photos and graphic images. The last tip I'll include about this is how to take an image with a complicated background, isolate it, copy it, and paste it into another image. There are several ways to do this but here is one way that works well with most images and is easy to explain.

Imagine a photo of a basket of fruit on a table with tapestry in the background. Lets say you wish to eliminate the background entirely so that only the basket of fruit can be seen and everything in the background is a solid color, often white.

If the background was a solid color you could use the magic wand selector tool and select the entire background. Then you could Cut the selected area to a new background color or Fill the background with a new color. But a complicated background like a tapestry, or one with graduated colors or tones, cannot be easily selected using the Magic Wand (color) selection tool. No matter how much the sensitivity tool is adjusted, the magic wand may select either too much or too little. If this happens try this to handle the problem.

Open the image and view it at 200%. Select the Paint Brush tool and choose a small size say four pixels. Choose a color like white that is different from the colors in the fruit basket. Carefully begin to paint around the outside of the fruit and basket.

Get as close as possible to the outline of the basket and continue until the basket is completely outlined with the small 4 pixel paint brush. Then choose a larger sized brush and repeat this process while being very careful not to paint into and over any part of the original image. Then use an even larger brush and paint out everything except the fruit and the basket. At this point the entire background should be white or some other solid color.

Next select the Magic Wand (selects by color) selection tool and set the sensitivity of 1 . Click once on the white background and all of the background should now be selected. Under the Select Menu, choose Inverse, and now the fruit basket is selected instead of the solid color background that you just created.. Choose Copy under the edit menu and then only the fruit basket (without the background) can be Pasted into another photo or blank window. This can be resized, rotated, distorted, or altered immediately using the appropriate Transform option under the Edit menu.

When you are happy with the way this looks, Deselect the fruit basket and Flatten the Image. There are other ways to do this but painting the background, selecting it with the magic wand, choosing the Inverse, and then copying this, and Pasting the image into another image or slightly larger window, is one method that always produces good results.

Then if you need to select the image again you can use the magic wand as before and paste one image without the background into another image. While this is still selected, you can resize it, move it, flip horizontal or vertical, change levels, contrast, etc. as you please.

If you wanted to select a complicated image like a close up of a girl with her hair blowing wildly in the wind, you would need to select her by Masking. Masking is an advanced technique and not needed to build profit center websites

Cutting an image with a complex background

1. open the image
and use the magnifying
glass tool to enlarge it
to 200% - 300%

2. carefully paint a solid
color (usually white)
around the fruit basket
with 4 pixel wide round
hard brush

3. paint around the
basket with a 15 pixel
brush

4. use a larger brush to
completely paint the
background then lower
magnification to 100%

5. select background
with magic wand tool
and select Inverse

6. cut or copy and
paste as desired, or
crop and save isolated
fruit basket photo

Chapter 8. Getting Started with Online Sales

eBAY.com

eBay is probably the most popular way to get started selling online. Quite a few people make their entire living selling on eBay and this is the most well known auction website in the country. It is a good way to test the market before you commit to carry new products on your profit center website. The site is easy to use and you'll know in a very short time if people are responding to your ad or not.

To get started you'll need a free eBay account and an easy way for customers to pay you online. Having a PayPal account works well for this as eBay actually owns PayPal.

You can list your item for auction and when the winning bidder pays you, you ship the product directly to the customer yourself or have it drop shipped. If you like you can put a reserve price on the item to protect you from losing money or you can put a buy it now price on the item so people don't have to wait for the auction to expire. eBay has good tutorial about selling on their website which makes it easy.

AMAZON.com

Amazon is well known for selling books and other items as well but you can sell your products through Amazon for a fee as little as 99¢ per sale plus other selling fees.

In addition they offer fulfillment services and they will actually ship your products for you if you like.

Since your product is being sold through Amazon, they handle the transaction and send you a check. Amazon has two ways to sell, one for professionals and one for individuals and will sell a wide variety of items for you according to their posted guidelines.

Some items require approval before they can be sold on Amazon and some categories of items are restricted. To see the lists, and find out more, click on Sell at the top of their home page.

Amazon is often the first place shoppers look for a huge variety of products. Their reach into the retail world is amazing and I have seldom if ever, found an item that they do not carry.

If for some reason you decide not to sell products on their site, it is a great place to check the competition who may be already selling on Amazon.

ETSY.com

Etsy.com is a popular site to sell handmade goods, vintage items, or craft supplies. They charge 20¢ to list an item for 4 months, or until it sells and a 3.5% fee on the sales price.

CRAIGSLIST.com

Craigslist.com has websites in many cities in the U.S. and allows users to post free classified ads with pictures. It is free and could be a good way to pre-test market products and various ad messages.

GETTING YOUR WEBSITE INDEXED ON SEARCH ENGINES:

Once you have a website you'll want to do a few things to promote it. Obviously you can always buy advertising too but this is one thing that you can do to promote your website without cost.

One of the first things to do is to register with the Search Engines. Google, Yahoo, and Bing, and AOL are the biggest. Just search for "Google add URL" or "Google submit site" and you will find instructions how to register your site with Google, and the other major search engines. It can take up to 6 weeks to get indexed in the Search engines so it is a good reason to do this right away.

Before you register with anyone be sure that your site contains keywords and meta tags that are relevant to your site or you will not be indexed. Search engines are looking for genuine content and guard against being scammed.

If you have "Pamela Anderson" listed as a keyword or meta tag, then your site better have something to do with Pamela Anderson or your site will not be listed. If you use text that is colored the same color as the background to fool the search engine while not being able to be seen by the page viewer, then your site will not be listed.

The biggest thing that contributes to a websites ranking by search engines is content. The more relevant content your site has, the higher it will be ranked,

Once you have registered manually for the big search engines you can register automatically with hundreds of others. Just search for free search engine submission to find companies that do this at no cost because they are hoping to sell you other services.

KEYWORDS:

It is important to mention that there are two types of keywords. The first type of keywords, as mentioned above, are those that are placed as Meta tags in the source code of every web page. These are the keywords that you hope people are searching for and this is how the search engine finds you whenever someone does a search.

The second type of keyword is used by some types of internet (paid) advertising companies and the more popular keywords and phrases generally cost more than those that have little interest.

Most companies that offer keyword advertising have their own free keyword research tool. These usually require (a free) registration before you can use their keyword tool. Once registered, they are easy to use. These tools work with a database that is derived from the searches that were made on one search engine and not all the search engines. Nonetheless the results can be expected to apply to other search engines as well.

First make a list of the keywords that you think might be good and type them one by one into the research tool. Then you can see a list of that keyword, and keyword phrases that people have searched for in the past and see how each word or search term ranks with the others. This will show you the search terms that people actually use on a regular basis.

LOOK AT COMPETITORS WEBSITES:

It is a good idea to take a look at some competitive websites to see how they look and feel. If you found your competition online by doing a search and then clicking on some of the top listings then your about to learn something.

Most web browsers will allow you to view the source code of a web page. Once you are looking at the code, the pictures and graphics will be gone and all that you will see is a page full of letters and numbers. Near the top of the page you will find the keywords and description meta tags used on the page. This will give you an idea of the kind of keywords that this site used to get a high page ranking. It is illegal to bulk copy another site's keywords but you can use the same words along with some others so that this is not a problem. As mentioned always be sure that your keywords are relevant to your website.

ADVERTISING YOUR WEBSITES:

If you have the money, you may want to pay for some advertising to get visitors to your website. One of the best ways to do this on a budget is to try Google Ad Words. This service allows you to buy ads which are based on keywords.

When someone searches for a keyword or phrase Google shows text ads (which are linked to that keyword) describing your website. When they click on the ad, this costs you a few cents and this amount is determined by your bid price on the keyword.

They allow you to set a budget so that you can control how much you want to spend on advertising . Even $50 or $100 a month in advertising could make a big difference in sales.

Some keywords are very expensive and can cost over a dollar each. Usually these high priced keywords won't be a problem for you unless you are selling gold coins or expensive items. In fact if you were selling a product with a model number, hardly anyone else will be bidding on this keyword so your cost will be as low as possible. Even an ad budget of $50 or $100 a month can make a big difference in traffic to your site.

Another website to consider keyword advertising at a lower cost is ExactSeek.com. They limit the number of advertiser's keywords to avoid overcrowding, and rotate the ads so that everyone purchasing a premium ad gets an equal number of exposures. Their premium ads appear across 90+ search engines and web directories and cost a flat rate of $4 per month per keyword or keyword phrase. With flat rate billing, they eliminate bidding for keywords, and pay-per-click advertising used by other companies.

If you search for "low cost website advertising" you will find many other companies with different advertising options. Several Internet advertising networks are listed in the resource section at the end of this book.

CONVERSION RATE:

Besides driving traffic to a website, one important part of selling things online is the conversion rate. This is the ratio of how many people visit a website over a specified time compared to how many of those people actually purchased something from your site. The average conversion rate is 2% - 4% and anything higher is outstanding.

For example, if you spent $100 on advertising your site for a month and attracted 500 visitors to your web site then a 2% conversion rate would result in 10 sales at a cost of $10 per sale. But if your conversion rate was 4% then this would result in 20 sales at a cost of $5 per sale.

Any effort than you devote to increasing your conversion rate will make a lot of difference in your bottom line. I like Google Ad Words and similar programs because the visitors are targeted by keywords.

I have heard that advertising with Google Ad Words for awhile will improve your overall page ranking on Google. It seemed to work for me, but I am not sure if this is really true or not.

Another type of paid internet advertising that is really cheap is untargeted ads. One company, EarnEasyCash.info, advertise a cost of 50¢ per 1000 visitors. Naturally the conversion rate will be lower from untargeted ads than from targeted ads.

CLASSIFIED ADVERTISING:

If you think that classified ads in print might do well for you, take a look at NationwideAdvertising.com . They offer all kinds of advertising deals for everything from large daily newspapers, to Thrifty Nickel and Pennysaver Ads, to College Newspapers. They have ad packages in many price ranges but one package for example will place your ad in 140 Pennysavers/Shoppers in ten States with a 3 million circulation for $249. This is less than $2 per classified ad!

I like print ads in papers like this because people tend to keep them around the house longer than daily papers and many people look through these several times before they are thrown away.

As mentioned earlier if you can craft an inexpensive classified ad that drives people to your website then you have the formula for success. With low ad costs like these, averaging only one sale per paper would result in a 140 sales at a cost of $249 so the ad cost per sale would be only $1.77.

TESTING AD COPY AND WEBSITE CONTENT:

If you are doing any advertising you should test your various ads to see which works best. First write the ad copy for the product you wish to test. Limit the number of words in the ad to make it as inexpensive to run as possible and then run the ad and measure the results over a three week period and record the sales that resulted from the ad.

Next run the same ad in the same place and change the headline of the ad. This is the first line and the line that grabs people's attention. Then record the sales results with headline #2. Repeat this with another headline and then chose the best of the three.

If there is no difference, keep the original headline and begin to test the description. Try testing this several times with various descriptions and record the results.

The last thing to test is what is known as the call to action. This is the part of the ad that makes the reader want to act and visit your website. You want to say something that makes the reader have a reason to act right away. You could try wording like, "Supply Limited – Order Now", "Newest Models and Lowest Prices", "Order Yours Today", or "Reserve Yours Today", etc. After 3 weeks you should have a pretty good idea about which combination of headline, description, and call to action ad copy produces the most sales for you.

It should be said that this is a very crude way to test classified ads on a low volume basis but you'll know a lot more if you test this way than if you don't test at all.

Web ads can be tested more thoroughly using additional criteria than just sales. Professional advertising companies can give you a better idea of the best use of your advertising dollars. This is much more accurate type of testing using a high volume number of ads, and different types of ads, and is used by companies with large advertising budgets.

Besides ad copy, you can also test various website designs to see which design, description, price, and call to action produces the best results. You will be able to view web statistics about your website traffic and tell a lot about how people arrive at your website and how long they stay on site and which pages they view.

It is difficult to tell how many people are visiting your website because of an ad unless you make a special page for this purpose. If your website URL is DogToysForActiveDogs.com and you include this URL in your ad, it is hard to determine who found you because of your ad.

Making a copy of the webpage that describes the product you are selling in the ad, and renaming it will solve this problem. For example if you advertise a renamed URL like DogToysForActiveDogs.com/deals.html then the only people that will ever visit this page are people that see this URL in your ad. Reviewing your website statistics you will know how many people visited the page from your ad and what sales occurred because of the ad.

This idea can be expanded by using different websites entirely instead of unique pages within a website. If you sold a variety of portable induction cooking appliances for example, you could have one website where prices gave you a 10% mark up, another website with the exact same products running a 15% mark up, and another clone website where your prices were marked up 20%.

Each of these sites would have a different domain name and URL and could be advertised without an extension added on the domain name. One website might have the domain InductionCooking.com, another might have the domain InductionCookingDeals.com, and the other might be CookingWithoutHeat.com.

This approach is a little more work, and costs a little more but it allows you to more easily test different prices and is better for advertising purposes.

SEARCH ENGINE OPTIMIZATION:

There are quite a few companies that claim that they can get you better ranking on search engines so that you get more traffic. I have never used a SEO company so I cannot give anyone firsthand advice about this. Admittedly I am the kind of person who would do the keyword research myself and then spend those advertising dollars elsewhere.

I understand that a good SEO company can be really useful when you are building a website so that it is friendly to the search engines from day one.

I also understand that it is possible for some shady SEO companies to actually lower or eliminate your sites ranking in a search engine. This is because some SEO companies use tricks like shadow domains and doorway pages to try to fool the search engines in order to improve page ranking and drive more traffic to the site. Once the search engines discover this, they will either lower your page ranking or blacklist the site from the search engine altogether.

In fact the latest news about Google is that they appear to be moving away from meta tag keywords to rank websites and instead are concentrating on website content.

SEO SOFTWARE:

If you are a do-it-your-self person you may want to look into trying some SEO software for yourself. Sometimes this is available through web hosts and called a SEO tool, so it won't cost anything to try. Some SEO software comes with a free trial period so you can try before you buy.

SEO software can be pricey but if you commit to learning how to use it, then it should pay for itself. Ranging from $200 - $500, today's modern SEO software concentrates on building and managing links, analyzing competition, researching keywords, and tracking performance.

Because of the steep learning curve and the testing time most readers will be better served finding new products and learning how to sell them than maximizing (free) search engine sales leads .

Q. What happens when you don't advertise?

FREE ADVERTISING FOR YOUR WEBSITE:

Up to now I have been talking about paid advertising. I like this best because you learn how to write better ads as you go and you don't have to wait very long to see the results.

There are many ways that you can advertise your website for free and some of these may make sense for you if you intend to keep the site for up over a year. You will be creating e-commerce websites and you will be generally be looking for more immediate results than can normally be achieved with most free advertising techniques.

Nonetheless here are a few ideas you can use to advertise your websites for free:

1) Use Social Media like Facebook, Twitter, YouTube, and Linkedin to boost sales.
2) Advertise your website using free classifieds
3) Keep in email contact with customers
4) Run reciprocal banner ads at 123banners.com
5) Offer discounts and special promotions to established customers
6) Make an effort to be known for excellent customer service
7) Send out a free press release using PRLog.org
8) Write a Blog or Newsletter to attract people to your websites.
9) Send a follow up "Thank You" message soon after their purchase is scheduled to arrive.

Answer: Nothing happens, nothing at all.

YOU ARE FREE TO SELL ALMOST ANYTHING:

Other than regulated products, you are free to sell anything that you like. Freedom is a great thing but sometimes in business freedom doesn't mean liberty, sometimes freedom can mean divorced from reality. You can find a way to sell almost anything if you WORK at it.

But I advise taking an easier approach. Sell what people already want and what they already use instead of trying to introduce something totally new.

Avoid products that need lots of demonstration. By selling items that people already want and are somewhat familiar with, your job is much easier since customers are pre-sold and basically looking for a good selection and price. No selling of the product is required and sellers simply need to carry the right product at an attractive price to capture a pre-sold buyer.

The bottom line is that it is easier to sell something that the customer already wants than something that they have not seen before. But if you want to try selling something new anyway, I encourage you. No matter what happens it won't cost much and you never know until you try.

But it is important to know when to pull the plug. Some people get so close to an item, and believe in it so much, that they never give up on it no matter what. A good business person knows when to cut their losses and declare a loser a loser and move on to another item that is easier to sell.

Remember that we will all have failures. The important thing is that we learn from them.

WEBSITE CHECK LIST

1. formally organize your business / get E.I.N. number
2. get business bank account + debit card. Open account with PayPal.com
3. decide what you want to sell
4. choose a domain name
5. sign up with a low cost web hosting company
6. get product pictures
7. put together website with shopping cart
8. add Meta tags + keywords
9. load up site + Test all links
10. register with search engines
11. advertise website
12. manage + fine tune the site
13. Start thinking about other products and website ideas

Chapter 9. The End of the Beginning

Lets face it. Most of us work because we have to. And for most of us, making money and earning a living is a chore, even a struggle. But making money can be fun if you approach it as a game. When you make a sale, you win, and most people find this satisfying and enjoyable.

If we are not consumed by the constant worry over paying monthly bills and providing for our family, turning your ideas into cash can be deeply rewarding. Seeing the virtual cash register ring can be stimulating as well, and this is always a great way to start the day.

Each time you open your inbox to discover that you have sold something and made a little money without trading your sweat or your time, you feel great. You feel successful because you started a business from scratch and now you are watching it make money. Unlike a wage earner who often feels used and tired when collecting his paycheck at the end of the week, you will feel empowered with every sale because this is celebrating your genius, your efforts, and your achievement.

To succeed in any game you must first learn the rules. It is learning the process of how to sell something that you don't make, to someone who you have never met, and making a profit doing this part time from home. Learning this process makes it all worthwhile. This knowledge can never be taken away from you and can work for you as long as you have the desire to make more money.

New ideas and new products will come and go, but once you know the process of testing ads and products, and how to sell online, you will be way better off than before you found this book.

YOU CAN MAKE MORE MONEY

KEEP A NOTEBOOK and MAKE A PLAN:

I have found it helpful to use a notebook to write my goals, plans, and lists using paper and a pen as opposed to recording lists on a computer. The reason this works for me is that I am not always near the computer and, by writing ideas down on paper, I am more likely to remember them.

I suggest getting a notebook, writing your ideas down and focusing on one product idea at a time. By keeping your notes in one hand written notebook, it will be easy to add new ideas that you may want to try in the future.

The nice thing about a list is that you can check off items that are completed and carry over tasks that are not quite finished.

When you get ideas about other products, websites, etc. you can record them in another section of your notebook so they are not forgotten. Keeping an old fashioned hard copy notebook is a good practice and will help you get organized. I hope that you enjoy the following poem by Douglas Malloch 1877–1938.

I have included this poem in this book because I have always enjoyed it knowing that it could have been written about me! It is difficult for most of us to self motivate since most work situations involve being told what to do. Written lists and plans for the day, really help since it is especially easy now to be distracted and waste what little creative time we have.

YOU CAN MAKE MORE MONEY

"If I Could Just Get Organized "

There may be nothing wrong with you,
The way you live, the work you do,
But I can very plainly see
Exactly what is wrong with me.
It isn't that I'm indolent;
Or dodging duty by intent;
I work as hard as anyone,
And yet I get so little done.
The morning goes, the noon is near,
And all around me, I regret,
Are things I haven't finished yet,
If I could only just get organized!
Not all that matters is the man;
The man must also have a plan.

With you, there may be nothing wrong,
But here's my trouble right along;
I do things that don't amount
To very much, of no account,
That really seem important though
And let a lot of matters go.
I nibble this, I nibble that,
But never finish what I'm at.
I work as hard as anyone,
And yet, I get so little done,
I'd do so much you'd be surprised,
If I could just get organized!

by Douglas Malloch

SELLING ONLINE FULLTIME:

Most people will use the ideas presented here in "You Can Make More Money" to generate additional money without getting a second job. Most of these people will want to keep their job and all the benefits like health insurance and retirement plans that go with it. Obviously there is a lot to be said for a regular paycheck that you can count on.

With Obamacare around the corner, company paid health care will be a huge benefit and will be coveted by employees.

However once a few profit centers start producing for you, then you will realize that it is possible to make more money than your regular job. Upon this epiphany you might be tempted to quit your job and sell online fulltime.

I urge you to resist this idea for a few months or more so that you are more financially secure before you make the move to fulltime self employment.

If you delay becoming a fulltime online seller for a few months or longer, you will be able to put all the profit you are generating from your websites back into your business and your business can grow faster.

Then you will be able to add more products, websites, and get more advertising if you can avoid taking any of the profit out of the business for awhile and work for the "man" just a little longer.

This being said, I have always been a strong proponent for being self-employed and selling online for the following reasons:

1) You have much more control of your life.
2) You are the boss. Nobody tells you what to do.
3) Success or Failure is in your hands. You have the ball.
4) You can travel or live anywhere you like as long as you have an internet connection.
5) You get many tax advantages over wager earners
6) You can work at home without commuting.

A WORD ABOUT SELLING & SALESMANSHIP:

Lots of people think that they could never sell anything because they are not salesmen. Maybe they don't relate well to people or maybe they think that if someone is making money, then someone else must be losing it.

The truth is that we all are involved in selling everyday whether we realize it or not. When you apply for a job you are trying to convince someone that you are a good worker and could be an asset to their company.

When we discuss politics we are selling our opinions. When you try to convince your spouse that you need a new car, this is selling too. Even deciding what to watch on TV is an act of selling.

When most people think of a salesman, they think of a slick talker who will try to talk them out of their money. Or maybe they think of a person who will stand on your foot and keep talking until you reach for your wallet.

I have been in sales one way or another for years and I can tell you that a salesman gets along with people in general and is not afraid to talk to them. But salesmanship is really a lot more than this.

Salesmanship is more about being a good listener so you can present the customer with what they want and need. It is about countering their objections to your product, and most important of all, salesmanship is about ASKING FOR THE MONEY and closing the deal. In short, salesmanship is just another skill that must be practiced and learned, and not a God given natural ability as some people think.

Although you won't have to be come a salesman or deal with people directly when selling online some understanding of the sales process will be helpful when you design your profit center websites and advertising campaigns. If enough customers ask about certain models, products, or special colors, listening to them and giving them what they want will end up making more money for you.

First your customer must want the product. This means that you need to do a good job showcasing it and describing its advantages and specifications. You can present various sizes of photos from different angles and post some testimonials or product reviews if you have them.

After your customer wants the product then they need to be assured that they are getting a deal, it will be shipped promptly, and that they should trust you with their credit card information.

When you receive an order from a customer, the order should be confirmed by you as soon as possible. You want your customer to KNOW that they have purchased the product and this understanding takes them out of the market.
This means that they are no longer shopping because they have already bought something. You don't want them shopping elsewhere or getting buyers remorse either, so an acknowledgement of their order seals the deal in their mind.

One more aspect of salesmanship is the follow through. A few days after your product has been delivered to the customer a good salesman will follow up with a phone call or an email to be sure that your customer likes the product. This makes people feel good about the company and they are more likely to remember this and recommend it to their friends.

YOU CAN MAKE MORE MONEY

BARTER KINGS:

Barter Kings is a TV reality show seen on A&E. This is a wonderful show for a couple of reasons and I do hope that you make an effort to see several episodes at least. If you do, it will show you how these two men can start with an item worth a few hundred dollars and five or six trades later have a boat or a car worth ten thousand dollars or more.

This show should be required viewing for anyone who is unemployed. By using Craigslist the men find something that they want for sale and visit the owner. If they still want it, they ask the owner why he is selling and usually it is because the owner wants or needs something else. Then the men explain that they think they can come up with exactly what the owner wants and then they try to find it, and trade for it.

In other cases they contact a seller and ask him if he would consider trading and if the seller says that he would consider it, they meet and try to make the trade.

This is where the show gets interesting. When they meet the owner they take a look at whatever he is selling and then show the seller whatever they have brought to trade. Usually the seller's item is worth lots more than what the Barter Kings have so the seller is reluctant to trade.

But by using strong sales abilities they usually make the trade. When the seller gripes about the discrepancy in value, the Barter Kings completely ignore this objection and ask the seller why he is looking for whatever they have in the first place. When this is known the Barter Kings keep reminding the seller of how their item will benefit him and how long the sellers item has been idle and just taking up space.

Then they offer to shake hands and say something like, "Well do we have a deal?. If the seller stalls, they remind him of the benefit again. If the seller still says no, the Barter Kings ask for the deal one more time, until the seller gives in and makes the trade.

I like the show because it illustrates how people can make money in a down economy and how good salesmanship can triumph when others would just give up. Once again it is well worth it to watch this show because it helps you learn how to become a better salesperson.

LISTEN TO YOUR ADVERTISING MESSAGE:

Years ago my wife and I were in the toy business and I learned an important lesson from her. I would be demonstrating how the toys worked and rapping my spiel to the crowd.

Our toys were reproductions of American Folk toys and many people were not familiar with them. I remember the day I learned to listen to the message that I was really communicating to the crowd. While pitching the toys I would say that these toys "used to be popular".

One day my wife was under our table, and out of the public's sight, and busy restocking the toys when she heard me say that our toys "used to be popular". Then she tugged at my pant leg and I watched her take $20 out of the cash box and slip it into her pocket while giving me a big smile. About $60 later I got the message.

I was telling the crowd that our toys USED TO BE POPULAR so the message I was giving the crowd was that nobody wants these toys anymore! Then I changed my pitch to, "These are reproductions of popular

118

American Folk toys" and this eliminated the subliminal negative and increased sales.

I mention this because it is important to examine our advertising and the way that we present our products so that we can eliminate as many negatives as possible. Consumers are defensive and naturally hesitant to act if there are any negative thoughts in their minds about the product, price, or the integrity of an online seller.

Especially now, people are concerned about sharing their credit card and personal info with strangers. Because of this justified paranoia, everything about your advertising and website design should inspire trust and encourage the customer to act (buy) now and not later. For this reason it is important to be careful about what your message is and how it is presented.

GONE FISHING:

For many reasons, business is a lot like fishing:

1) You can't catch any fish if you don't go fishing.
2) People who go fishing catch more fish than people who don't.
3) You can't catch any fish until you have some bait in the water.
4) Mostly you catch small fish but every now and then you'll catch some really big fish too.
5) You don't stop fishing just because you haven't caught any fish.
6) Sometimes the fish aren't biting and there is nothing you can do about it.
7) Changing the bait can produce more fish

8) Going fishing is fun whether you catch any fish that day or not.
9) Hooking the fish and reeling it in is fun but netting the fish and getting it into the boat means that you'll have a fish to eat.

BON VOYAGE:

Thanks to the advent of low cost web sites and the idea of building small profit centers (that can pay off monthly for years) you should be well on your way to being your own boss and controlling your own destiny.

The trend in e-commerce is in your favor. According to InternetRetailer.com U.S. online sales will grow at an annual rate of 10% per year from now to 2017. Global e-commerce is growing at an even faster rate at more than 19% a year. While other industries are dying or just treading water, e-commerce is trending toward growth ranging from robust to sensational for at least the next five years.

A man once said to me, "I hear that you reap what you sow. What have you been sowing lately?

"Not a Damned Thing", I thought to myself. This changed my life.

Hopefully this book and these ideas will change your life as well. In the words of Star Trek's Mr. Spock, "Live long and prosper my friends".

YOU ARE ON YOUR WAY

Now that you have your
first webstore up and running,
you can start thinking about
the next one.

YOU CAN MAKE MORE MONEY

WEB and ADVERTISING TERMS:

Above the Fold: regarding banner ad placement, this refers to a banner ad on a web page that can be seen without scrolling down or across the page.

Ad Networks: are companies that sell advertising on a cost per thousand, cost per click, or cost per action basis.

Ad Views: the number of times an ad has been displayed and usually purchased on a cost per thousand basis.

Ad Rotation: web ads that are plugged into available spaces on a rotating basis allowing for several advertisers to be seen in the same ad space.

Affiliate Marketing: involves the sale of another website's products or services

Anchor text: the visible text in a hyperlink

Animated GIF: this is a graphic image made up of layers that display in a timed sequence to provide animation and the illusion of motion.

Average markup: the difference between what you paid for total merchandise sold in a specific time period and what you sold this for, expressed as a percentage.

Backlink: incoming links to a website.

Banner: A graphic advertisement used on websites.

When clicked this is usually linked to another website, web page, or email address.

Bandwidth: the amount of data that can be sent through a computer connection in a given time period.

Bridge page: a web page that is designed to rank well with search engines and is linked to another web page or website.

B2B: is called business to business and means that a company is targeting business (commercial) customers instead of consumers.

B2C: business to consumers -businesses that target retail consumers

Bleed: a printing term that means printing right to the edge of the paper without a margin.

CGI: common gateway interface – small scripts or programs that run on web pages and are stored at the same location as the website.

Classified Advertising: print ads arranged by category.

Click: when a person reacts to an advertisement by clicking on it.

Click stream: the trail of pages that a user visits when navigating one or more websites.

Click rate: the percentage of ad views that resulted in the viewer clicking on the ad.

Cookie: a file on a users hard drive that allows a website to record data about the user. Often these are used to insure that the user is presented with different banners and ads every time they visit the site.

CPM: a cost per thousand ad payment plan is a business model where advertisers pay a fee that is based on the number of times that their ad was displayed.

CPA: cost per action - a business model where advertisers pay only when a person responds to the ad and buys the product or registers for a drawing or newsletter, etc.

CPC: cost per click - a business advertising model where advertisers pay based on the number of times that people clicked on the ad.

CPS: cost of advertising on a per sale basis

DBA: doing business as – the name a company uses for its business that is distinct from the registered name of the business. Example: JoeBlow, Inc. dba: Joes Dog Toys

Demographics: The characteristics of a group or audience based on age, culture, income, etc.

Display Advertising: Ads composed of both graphics and print designed to attract more attention than classified ads.

Domain name: the unique name (and number) for a website that distinguishes itself from other websites.

DNS: domain name server – a system that stores information using a shared database to provide an IP address for each host name and lists the email servers accepting email for each domain.

Drop Ship: when a seller who wholesales products to other sellers and ships them to the customers on behalf of the seller.

EPV: earnings per visitor

Frames: an html extension that divides web pages into separate and distinct areas where text and image content can be inserted.

FTP: file transfer protocol – a method used to transfer files from one computer to another using the internet.

Fulfillment: getting your product in the hands of your buyer so that they are satisfied with the transaction.

Html: hyper text mark up language: a formatting code that tells web pages how to display text with different fonts, sizes, color, styles, etc.

Hyperlink: or link is a reference in a (hypertext) document to another web page or website.

Image map: a defined part of a picture on a web page that is active so that when someone clicks on this, it results in an action like replacing the picture, or going to another web page.

IP address: a unique number used by computers to identify each other when exchanging information.

ISP: an internet service provider

JPG: or jpeg – a type of image file that reduces image size and download time by using various levels of compression.

Keystone markup: the retail practice of doubling the cost to arrive at a retail price.

Keyword: a word that is searched for in a search command.

Keyword phrase: search terms using more than one keyword.

Meta tag: a protocol that provides data about the data on a web page including title, description, + keywords.

Mirror site: an exact copy of a website often used by sites that provide large downloads.

Page rank: the order that web pages come up when using a search engine.

Pay per click: when advertisers pay a set amount each time that a person that clicks on their ad whether they buy or not

Popup: an ad that displays in a separate window when a new web page is called up.

Run of Site: a run of site ads will display throughout the site in different locations on a rotating basis.

SEO: search engine optimization – a methodology to improve search engine page rankings of websites based on keywords.

Target group: the group of people that advertisers target.

Trim size: the final size of a book, poster, or magazine page after it is trimmed.

Traffic: the amount of data sent and received by website visitors.

SSL: provides secure communication on the internet. Usually used with shopping carts which handle sensitive information like credit card numbers.

Unique visitor: this is used to measure how many new people visit a website in a specified time period. If they return to the site during the specified period, they are only counted as a new person once during this time period.

URL: uniform resource locator – or web address of a web page. This usually contains an extension of the domain name to bring up a specific page, within the domain. Example:www.BigTime Deals.com/clocks.html is the URL for only one page within the BigTimeDeals.com domain.

Visits: the number of times unique visitors view a website in a specified time period.

Web Host: a company that provides disc space to house websites.

Whois: this is a protocol that allows you to determine who owns a domain or IP network.

WYSIWYG: what you see is what you get – this term refers to the fact that most modern word processors and web page editors display the page while hiding control characters so that the page appears, acts. or prints almost exactly as you see it on the screen.

Resources for Online Sellers

Please note that the following websites and URL's were verified at the time of publication. However it is likely that, over time, some of these websites will no longer be operating. If you find this to be the case, then search for other similar websites and I am sure that you'll find some good ones. My Google search for "drop shippers" yielded over 800,000 results. All URL's listed below start with http://www.

ONLINE SELLERS & AUCTION SITES

1) eBay.com
2) Amazon.com
3) Etsy.com
4) Webstore.com
5) eBid.net
6) OnlineAuction.com
7) ePier.com
8) eCrater.com

DROP SHIPPERS & DROP SHIP DIRECTORIES

1) CafePress.com
2) Doba.com
3) DHGate.com
4) Shopster.com
5) Dropshipsites.com
6) Simplx.com
7) Megagoods.com

SOME LOW COST HOSTING COMPANIES

1) 1dollar-webhosting.com
2) iPage.com
3) Justhost.com
4) Fatcow.com
5) Bluehost.com
6) Hostmonster.com
7) Web.com
8) Volusion.com
9) Homestead.com
10) 1and1.com

ADVERTISING ON MAJOR SEARCH ENGINES

1) Bing.com
2) Yahoo.com
3) Google.com
4) Aol.com
5) MSN.com
6) AltaVista.com

SOME INTERNET ADVERTISING NETWORKS

1) Clickbank.com
2) Tradedoubler.com
3) Admedia.com
4) Adbrite.com
5) Bidadvertiser.com
6) Advertising.com
7) Infolinks.com

YOU CAN MAKE MORE MONEY

SOME PAYMENT PROCESSORS

1) PayPal.com
2) 2checkout.com
3) Authorize.net
4) Ccnow.com
5) Mercantec.com

SOME BOOK, eBOOK, & DVD PUBLISHERS

1) Blurb.com
2) CreateSpace.com
3) Lulu.com
4) Xlibris.com
5) CafePress.com
6) Bookbaby.com
7) Infinitypublishing.com
8) Publishgreen.com

WEBSITES FOR ARTISTS AND DESIGNERS

1) Zazzle.com
2) CafePress.com
3) FineArtAmerica.com

FREE KEYWORD SEARCH TOOLS:

1) Google.com/sktool/
2) Freekeywords.wordtracker.com
3) Keyworddiscovery.com/search.html

LISTS OF ESTABLISHED WEBSITES FOR SALE

1) Websitebroker.com
2) Flippa.com
3) Latonas.com
4) Ebizbrokers.com

About the Author

Nearly twenty years ago Steve Long was driving back to Idaho from an art show in Bozeman, Montana. It was nearly one hundred degrees and his van was running hot. Without AC the windows were open and the heater was running full blast, but the temperature gauge was still nearly pegged. With two hours of daylight left, Steve was dying in the heat until he heard a radio show that took his mind off his misery. The show was about the internet and how webmasters could earn $100 per hour working from home.

The Internet was in its infancy then but Steve jumped into web work with both feet and has been doing graphic work and making web pages and websites ever since. For over ten years he has operated a very successful website and continues to do so today.

He points out that people have a unique opportunity today to make money online that did not exist in the past. Now we can have our own websites for only a few dollars a month, hundreds less than even a few years ago.

Thanks to easy to use software, even casual computer users can learn to build and operate online profit center websites. Steve encourages his readers to start their own businesses and operate multiple profit centers, which when added together, can produce a significant monthly income. Steve says, "It doesn't matter whether you are young or old. If you can use a computer to send emails and surf the web, you can learn how to make money online."